THE DARK GLASS

Meditations in Orthodox Spirituality

Mother Thekla

Fount
An Imprint of HarperCollins*Publishers*

F
30
146

To Marilyn Wood,
a dear friend of the Monastery for many years

Fount Paperbacks is an Imprint of
HarperCollins*Religious*
Part of HarperCollins*Publishers*
77–85 Fulham Palace Road, London W6 8JB

First published in Great Britain
in 1996 by Fount Paperbacks
1   3   5   7   9   10   8   6   4   2

Copyright © Mother Thekla 1996

Mother Thekla asserts the moral right to be
identified as the author of this work

A catalogue record for this book is
available from the British Library

ISBN 0 00 628004 8

Printed and bound in Great Britain by
Woolnough Bookbinding Limited, Irthlingborough,
Northamptonshire

CONTENTS

FOREWORD

This is an unusual book, and it was written in an unusual place. In one of her other works, Mother Thekla has herself described the setting of the Orthodox Monastery of the Assumption at Normanby, near Whitby, where she lives and writes: '... the bleakest strip of the coast in north-east Yorkshire, a strip so windblown that it is always three weeks behind in any harvesting, not behind the rest of England, but the rest of Yorkshire!'[1] Yet the setting, if bleak, is also strikingly beautiful: placed some 600 feet above sea level, the Monastery commands wide-ranging views in one direction across the North Sea, and on the other side across the empty expanses of the North York Moors. It has the character of an 'end-point', to use a term often employed by the founder of the Monastery, Mother Maria (1912–1977) – '*my* Mother Maria', as Mother Thekla calls her.

1 Sister Thekla, *Mother Maria: Her Life in Letters* (Darton, Longman & Todd, London 1979), p. xxxvii.

Something of the austerity of the Monastery's physical situation is reflected in Mother Thekla's spiritual outlook, with its clarity and integrity, its refusal to compromise, its rigorous yet generous compassion. The pages that follow likewise reflect the hillside at Normanby in their largeness of vision, in their broad and all-embracing scope.

One of the master-themes recurring throughout Mother Thekla's reflections on the Gospel of St Matthew – a leitmotif which I personally found especially helpful – is the way in which faith and doubt, so far from being mutually exclusive, need to coexist in the life of the Christian. Here Mother Thekla follows the teaching of her own spiritual mother. 'God in his goodness,' writes Mother Maria, 'gave us his word in a form which does not exclude doubt … I wonder if faith *inside* continued doubt, and the *bare* enduring of doubt, *is* not faith in its most tender and true humility.'[2]

Such exactly is the viewpoint which Mother Thekla endorses throughout her book. 'We, as human beings, cannot avoid doubt,' she writes; 'doubt is no sin, nor does it mean that we are deserted. Far from it: in doubt we are drawn into the divine suffering.' Thomas was not blamed but blessed for his doubt, Mother Thekla points out; doubt, so far from being an

2 *ibid.*, pp. 10, 48.

enemy, is often the 'way in' to a living faith. Indeed, faith and doubt are inseparable; 'If no doubt, no faith.'

In all this, Mother Thekla is in no way advocating scepticism or relativism as an ultimate position. On the contrary, she believes fiercely in the absolute nature of God's truth: 'In our earthly realm all is relative: in the divine, all is absolute.' But at the same she insists that faith functions on a level entirely different from the proofs and systems based on human logic. Faith means, not logical certainty, but a personal relationship: it is inseparable from warm, living personal love, from love towards a person – faith is a personal presence, the presence of Christ himself.

Mother Thekla urges us, when studying Scripture, to read the words as if we were listening to them for the very first time, 'as a child might do.' Her commentary on the Gospel of St Matthew, characterized as it is by a sharp focus and a startling freshness, will help us to achieve exactly that.

Timothy Ware,
Bishop Kallistos of Diokleia
Oxford, July 1996

PREFACE

MY APPROACH to the Gospel of St Matthew, as will become only too obvious, is entirely untheological – as we understand a theological exposition. I am concerned with only one aspect which I find continually new and absorbing: the pre-eminent place given to doubt as the foundation for the work of the spirit.

The contradictions even within the one Gospel are manifold. And, again and again, they seem to me to point to the limitations of the human mind and to warn us against asserting any absolute value to any mortal condition, seemingly good or seemingly bad.

Throughout this short scrutiny of the Gospel of St Matthew, I am suggesting that the greatest profit would appear to lie, not in attempting to ignore or iron out the contradictions, but to accept them gladly as the basis of faith.

I have taken the subjects in alphabetical order since this would seem the only way to avoid even the appearance of evaluating what may not be evaluated.

INTRODUCTION

A Note on Orthodoxy

HOW IS IT THAT I DARE to write some kind of introduction to the Orthodox attitude of faith? I am not a theologian, nor a Church historian – I am simply an Orthodox nun. Is that possibly the clue?

And here is another possible clue: When Mother Maria, the founder of our abbey in England and my spiritual mother, wrote her *Hidden Treasure*, she gave it to a scholarly priest for his observations: he read the book with great interest but suggested that she should give her references to the Fathers whom she had quoted. Mother Maria said nothing. The answer was simple – she had not read them as a preparation for her book – nor was the *Hidden Treasure* a distilled version of any of the Fathers of the Church *specifically*. I say *specifically* because the Fathers held and preserved and were martyred for the Tradition which each one of us, from the wisest to the simplest, inherits and preserves according to our capacity.

What is this Tradition, which, even unconsciously,

is our personal heritage, our foundation of faith, the basis for so much of our daily working tradition?

First and foremost, I suggest that the gap, whatsoever gap there is, between us and the West, lies fundamentally in our approach to the Holy Spirit. For us, the Holy Spirit has nothing to do with the century or place in which we happen to live. The Holy Spirit has nothing to do with contemporary or local morals, or with the lack of them, in an 'enlightened' view of sex or murder, in up-to-date aspects of psychology or education or contemporary language – or, in fact, in anything reflecting essential worldly changes from generation to generation, changes based on fresh scientific experiment in every sphere of daily life.

Our Holy Spirit is a person – a Person of the Holy Trinity – who, *in spite* of worldly change, fashion, and 'progress', keeps us steadfastly with one foot, if not both feet, in the mystical place where time and eternity meet. Our Holy Spirit *denies* that truth can alter from one generation to another: denies the claim of human *knowledge*. Our Holy Spirit is as inscrutable, unknowable, untouchable as the Father Himself. He is the antidote to all that is immanent and transient. He is the divine answer to every temptation of the Devil towards the confusion of the spiritual goal with the material – Love and love: God and man. The Holy Spirit is the essence of martyrdom: the power, the courage, the audacity to persist against all fashion in putting God first, and man second. The Holy Spirit, if I may put it like that, is our balance against the human arrogance which still seeks, as its right, a paradise on earth. And so we come to the mystery of suffering.

One inherited facet of Orthodoxy is the rejection of happiness as a *right*. This does not mean that in actuality we do not seek to alleviate suffering, but we object to an attitude which demands unadulterated worldly contentment. We cling to the rejected temptation of Christ in the wilderness – He refused once and for all a worldly paradise – and above all in contradiction to worldly bliss we hold to the eternal mystery of the Cross. Somehow – we do not know *how* specifically, but somehow – suffering is blessed. The Russian tendency to see anyone in total wretchedness as particularly chosen of God, the Russian compassion for prostitutes and pity for the condemned criminal in chains on his long trek to Siberian exile, stems somehow from the positive identification with any kind of suffering within the Christian Tradition … Mentally defective people, fools, vagabonds, outcasts of any kind demand our pity first and foremost because, and not in spite of, their having rejected or not found the spirit of truth. Not only is judgment forbidden us but grief for the felon takes its place. Sentimental? Perhaps. In some instances overdone. But yet – the refusal to judge according to the judgment of the world – the Holy Spirit, the spirit of truth, the spirit of understanding working within each one of us.

The Tradition … but how do we seek to keep inside this Tradition? We can only work on a very small scale in our daily lives. Thus in the knowledge of the Holy Spirit, in the knowledge of the *Tradition*, we help ourselves and bring to our aid all the even apparently unimportant facets of tradition. The little things which could be considered simply contemporary or 'decorative' we use as our aids to holding to *the* Tradition. We refuse *change* on the principled grounds that once the door is opened to change, more and more changes will tumble over each other in the hope of keeping up with the fashion of the new generation – more and more absorption in human rights as opposed and even diametrically contrary to the holding fast to the one unchanging truth.

Once we throw out Tradition by ignoring tradition, however unfashionable and even comical it might seem, we are opening the floodgates to divert the current of our attention to happiness, contentment, satisfaction, fulfilment, all diametrically opposed to the facing of Christ in our naked poverty. Hence we avoid change, or at least we try not to change, and if we do we make excuses for such change on the level of human necessity rather than justifying such change by accusing the Holy Spirit of such innovation.

But how can I begin even to be more explicit about this mystery of tradition in the Orthodox daily life? We have the tradition of the ikons: the belief that Christ Himself blessed the first ikon, that we should always have the presence of God and His mother and His saints among us. Representing the communion of saints – no barricade between the living and the dead, one communion – the ikons bring the comfort of unity and the knowledge that we need never feel lonely. We need never feel forsaken or deprived of the Eternal in our immanent lives – we are not cast adrift on the stormy waters of ever-changing human values. Our ikons hold us steadfastly on the frontier of life and Life – the divine hand stretched out to Peter. And with the help of the ikons we are vividly, constantly, made aware that there is the *one* communion – the dead supplicate for us, even as we intercede for them. We continue to love our dead even as we loved them in life and they lie in the earth among us after they have their last Liturgy with us in church – no decorous funeral parlours!

And, as with ikons, which must be painted *inside* the Tradition without personal idiosyncratic contemporary deviations, so too with our music: no instruments – only the human voice in worship – only the music of the eight tones handed down from generation to generation. And so too the actual expression of our faith – the words of worship – how true they must remain as the verbal manifestation of the truth within human limitations. One serious problem is the rich multiplicity of English and the temptation to use doctrinal and theological terms where in the original no such fine distinction obtains. Christ, our God, in the Thrice Holy Hymn of the Orthodox, sung or said, surely is *deathless* rather than *immortal* – we are not proclaiming a dogma but a faith.

Even the worship in church for the Orthodox has its traditional pattern, or rather, lack of regimented pattern. We stand before Christ, hurrying to Communion as the crowd beset Him, no question of directed disciplined queues! There are no pews – the whole church heaven on earth where we are free to wander, to greet the saints whom we love in the ikons, and to listen to the singing – ever within the communion of saints, the living and the dead, as we light candles for those we love, alive and dead. Every word of the services remains unchanged – except, unhappily, a few somewhat idiosyncratic English translations! Greek and Slavonic merge comprehensibly and otherwise! Wheresoever there is an Orthodox service, the language is of least importance, we know exactly where we are if we are familiar with any 'Orthodox' language.

No change: for us that is the pre-eminent work of the Holy Spirit. Hold to the truth, however inadequately. Avoid human interference in the divine, in the vain seeking to make the incomprehensible comprehensible, the assigning of human logical reasoning over the unreasonable *Logos*.

Our Orthodox faith is a living faith. This cannot be said too often to a generation which sees a faith in harness with changing times. The Holy Spirit is active now – and the now is for us the self-limitation of the Eternal into the temporal: a manifestation of divine generosity. Only through the Spirit can we keep alive the teaching of Christ. And here, perhaps, I should make something clear which for us needs no elucidation.

The teaching of Christ: Only the Gospel Book is carried into the church at the Entrance in the Liturgy: only the Gospel Book is venerated – kissed reverently – even as an ikon. Perhaps in one sense *the* ikon: the Ikon of the Incarnate Word. For the Orthodox, the term *theology* does not suggest the discussion of the Gospel but its exposition. There is no place for the delving into manuscripts to discover disparity of accounts, and, hence, grounds for and against aspects and expressions of creed. Our dogma was defined in blood and martyrdom hundreds of years ago and embodied in the decrees of the Councils. It is perhaps even frighteningly simple for the intelligent or academic observer – for us, theology is the expression of the Word of God. Christ *is*. Either we believe, or are prepared to strive to believe, or not.

Human argument cannot give a firmer foundation to faith – it can only undermine faith by controversial logic. We cannot prove God. The Gospel is the ultimate divine mystery and not an aid to, nor, indeed, basis for religious argument. In fact, it emphasizes contradiction. How Christ's murderers longed for a sign so that He might be spared – how the Devil tempted Christ in the wilderness to give proof of His divinity. And He refused. God demands *faith*.

As Orthodox, in principle, we acknowledge the limitations of human reason even if we, as all humanity, cannot live up to our conviction. We know that we must not demand proof of Christ's divinity – we know that there are glaring contradictions in the gospel accounts. We know that it can probably be proved, and has been, that St John did not write the Apocalypse. We know and we rejoice: if we can no longer be martyred for our faith, we can at least gladly bear the stigma of being wholly irrational and impervious to proven facts. We will not be pushed into applying bounds of human reason to the inscrutable divine. We will not argue on the level of human debate. We are not concerned with pedantic historical investigation. It is hard enough work in our daily lives to follow Christ's teaching without discussing His validity.

However, this leads on to another aspect of daily Orthodoxy. There is a lighter side – all the fun of fasting and feasting. Perhaps the fasting, in non-Orthodox countries, is the greater fun. On the whole, we have lost a little of the fundamental concept of fasting and hence the necessity for the poverty of food during fasting times, and the disregard of interesting dishes whatever their ingredients. The basic concept of *ignoring* our appetites in all directions during times of fasting whether in the form of actual food, or entertainment, or conjugal bliss, has somewhat deteriorated in practice if not in theory.

In the West, where 'fasting' food is in no way a normal poor diet – the requirement for fish on Friday, for example – it can all too easily become an exotic adventure where octopus may be substituted for cod, and caviare or lobster for crab paste! The aim for the 'right' ingredients is hardly a Lenten restriction on the senses! And yet perhaps the dietary pastime has its Orthodox connotation, for, whatever else, we cannot be accused of common sense. And even as we drink our soya in the place of milk, eat black in the place of white chocolate, and ignore the small print wherever we can throughout Lent, we do pray for forgiveness, even more assiduously than at other times.

And so to a most important emphasis in Orthodox spirituality – repentance.

Ever and again morality is the direct enemy of spirituality, in effect, of Christianity – the work of the Holy

Spirit in each of us. Morality – kindness, generosity to the poor, hospitality, not stealing, nor murdering, visiting the sick, all that is admirable – may well be a diabolic delusion for it may remain on the level of *behaviour*. It may well remain the fulfilment of the Law. The spirit may be in barren idleness while the good works soothe and delude – the spirit may be not only idle but deeply troubled.

Spiritual indolence, particularly under the veneer of kindness and generosity and hospitality, can only be combated by repentance – prostration before God in an acknowledged inadequacy. *Repentance* – repentance for our spiritual wretchedness and limitations, our straitened hearts, our layers of righteousness: we fast, we go to church, we are at peace with our colleagues. Repentance is a moving inner force of traditional Orthodox spirituality – not remorse for a particular sin or wicked action, not penitence for some moral or ecclesiastical omission – but, sheer, naked *repentance*: contrition for the sin of the heart, a sin which can hardly be defined and remains the most vicious in the spiritual life of the Christian. Hence the importance of the *Jesus Prayer* in our Tradition.

The *Jesus Prayer* is the prayer of the heart to face the sin of the heart: the concentration on the Name, the Person of God the Son, God Incarnate, so that no room remains for anything else but Him alone, that evil may be replaced inch by inch and there is no empty room to welcome in a larger group of devils. Of course, such inner cleansing of the sinful soul is unattainable and so there is no alternative but unceasing repentance. Repent, and again repent. Such repentance in the cry of the heart casts out fear as we lie prostrate before our beloved Saviour. The *Jesus Prayer* is positive, and, as we repeat His Name over and over and over again, we find the peace of His presence – the precious pearl which gives us the wealth of the hope of salvation.

By way of the *Jesus Prayer*, we find ourselves at another point of fundamental Orthodox attitude: we are not at home in constricting legal analysis, in doctrinal terms for basic points of faith. We hold fast to the *mystery*. As regards salvation – what can we, with our human minds, know of divine providence, of divine judgment, of divine goodness? There can be no human definitions, but simply the demand for blind faith outside man's fumbling to make comprehensible what may not be comprehended. Our theologians throughout the centuries, if not pushed too far by heresy, *expound* the Gospels, and do not *discuss* them.

I once knew a Cypriot priest who decided to attend an English theological university course with the purpose of attaining an English academic degree. After a few weeks he left the college. I asked him why he had given up so soon. In total disdain of such 'heresy', his scornful reply was: 'I will not have Christ touched.' All his life he had been spared vain debates: his theology was the expounding of Christ, not considering His validity as God. On the whole we do not identify heretical innovation with traditional doctrine. Perhaps we need to be even more cautious now that we are more open to Western influence and its tradition of free doctrinal discussion. Freedom, yes. But not Renaissance humanism.

We should be led instead towards prayer, meditation, the saints. A word perhaps is necessary on our attitude to our saints. St Seraphim tamed the wild animals around his hermit seclusion. St John Chrysostom died for the true faith. If St Seraphim's status is clear, what is St John's? Martyr? Father of the Church? Or both? Our saints, our holy ones, are not put into categories.

There is only one important word here, holy. Saint, in English, has a legal connotation: the Church bestows as it were a legal acknowledgment of the holiness – human honour to sanctity even as a knighthood to a politician. Our holy ones emerge as it were in their own chosen way: a miracle, a vision, a growing popular demand for veneration of the relics. Of course this may open the way to superstition and abuse, but what does not? And who are we to deny the grain of truth that yet may linger in the worst abuse of popular gullibility?

Superstition is certainly one of the most unpleasant manifestations of our Orthodox faith and it is not improved by Western Orthodox who on the whole have not the capacity for cynical disbelief to live in tranquil companionship with sincere or credulous belief as they might well do in the Russian soul. For the Western mind it is not easy to absorb the brazen dialectic of the Eastern. And, without the capacity to believe and not believe, to scoff and accept, to respect our bishops and ignore any behest not to our liking, to delight in the glory of the Liturgy and never be there on time, without all this, and far more, Orthodoxy, as it is *lived*, may well be a problem for the more decorous West. And we, on our part, should not deny our heritage of freedom, illiterate and corrupt as we may be, in favour of the new Orthodox who, in more ways than one, may still cling, even unknowingly, to their own inherited tradition.

It is of no use to blow our spiritual trumpets, and, to mix metaphors, crow over the West that we have never had a Reformation: it is no good to proclaim that we alone are the true Church. We believe and pray that we are, or, at least, part of it, in heaven's estimation, but we certainly, however much some of us might wish to do so, cannot *prove* it. We know it for ourselves, but who are we to judge what goes on over the fence in a neighbouring church? We are somewhat inclined, as steadfast Orthodox, to judge what we know very little about – a hackneyed phrase, *'unlike the West'*. It might be more spiritually valuable if we concentrated on ourselves, on beams in our own eyes rather than motes in others! And, above all, if we – in spite of all the difficulties – kept to the validity of the person rather than absorbing the world in criticizing other Christians.

Christ was a Person on earth – a Person divine and human, and we are called to be persons: not just pieces of dough in a massive human lump. In the days before television, there were journals and newspapers, with individual opinions, political or religious or social. Literate members of society could, with their chosen periodical, assimilate a particular outlook. People, in effect, differed in their mental diet and were offered and could feed upon a wide vista of opinion. But, now, all see the same news on television, hear the same propaganda, watch and hear the same as millions of others – without contradiction, or only the contradiction served up to them. The human mind is being drained of the contradictions essential for creative human thinking and evaluation of situations. Insidiously, individuality is being sapped of its personal liberty. We are being trained to think the same, talk the same language distilled to the 'politically correct' – no longer permitted to be 'blind' but forced into 'visually challenged', a condition which evokes no immediate compassion, nor Christ's divine pity. We cannot even eat, without all reading the same nonsensical food ingredients on the tin and the inevitable 'best before …' Supermarkets

– no grocer, no ironmonger, no baker. Computers. Answering machines. What are we to do?

What is the Christian answer to the demonic annihilation of the individual, whether it be individual suffering, the mentally deficient child no longer pitied as such, or individual preference for English milk rather than European? What is the answer to this horrifying mask making all our faces one? Is there any hope of remaining persons and not organized dummies?

Surely the answer lies in the Gospels as it has throughout all the years of heresy and persecution. If the Gospels could survive assault on every religious level, cannot they, even now, give the answer to a materialism which sickens even those whom it corrupts? How can the Gospels answer the eminently reasonable anti-spiritual ethos of society? Surely only in being left austerely outside this area of disputation in human terms – in remaining for us *un*-reasonable, *ir*-rational, *un*-provable. Each one of us is the Church, and each one of us must keep his individuality, a living flame, if only in refusing one tiny aspect of undigested world. Martyrdom? I doubt it. We are far too tolerant. But we should expect some suffering over such unscholarly attitude to the Gospels. What does the truth matter, well we may ask, as long as there are footnotes?

Ultimately, however, how does it all add up? What have we as Orthodox Christians to offer? We are very far from perfection and perhaps our worst inclination is towards overpiety spilling over into superstition, and devout veneration verging on idolatry. Not so long ago, I was delighted by a manifestation of simple devotion. A friend of the monastery, a geologist, wandering over the sands of Whitby, came upon a very large ammonite which he presented to us. Somehow it never got moved from the table where he put it outside the church. Not long afterwards I came upon a woman solemnly venerating the ammonite as a precious rock from the Holy Land and, on seeing me, eagerly asking for its sacred origin. I am afraid that I disillusioned her. And then – I wondered. Well may St Hilda have trodden on this ammonite even as St Peter on the rocks of Palestine.

The communion of saints: the *mystery* of the communion – how can I know where the saints have trodden, where they have blessed? And I remember my Mother Maria again and her serene conviction that in heaven 'we walk in and out of each other' – no more divisions of body and soul, suspicion and estrangement. The fire of hell? What of the burning fire of Love whose penetration we cannot endure if we have not opened out our hearts to our finite capacity during our life on earth? There is a constant need to practise the opening of our hearts, even to suffering the assaults of evil, of injustice.

I began with the words, which she lived in her life, of my Mother Maria and so before I finally describe my approach in the Gospel thoughts that follow, I shall end this introduction with her – working no doubt in heaven as hard as she worked on earth – because I am as sure as I can be of anything, that in heaven she continues to smile at my rash inadequacies and somehow transform them to something passable if not adequate.

So – to sum up: the following thoughts are really only concerned with one aspect of the Gospel of St Matthew, the 'contradictions' which are the basis for a working faith and not a scholastic resolution of doubt. I am suggesting that the greatest profit for the everyday Christian, not the theologian as the term is normally understood, is not in the impossible task of attempting to iron out the contradictions, but to grasp them gratefully as a lifeline to *faith* – the joy that the final resolution to immanent contradiction lies beyond us – awaits us – beyond this realm where we can only see darkly.

I have taken the gospel subjects under their simplest headings and in alphabetical order since this appears to me a sensible way of avoiding any semblance of evaluation on my part. No evaluation of the divine by the human, and, even further, no limited time or space for the divine. Hence, the epitome of the Orthodox approach to the events, the feasts of the Church. For us, in our services, there is no use of the past tense: the feast day is not the *remembrance* of an event hundreds of years ago, it *is* the event.

Today the Holy Mother of God falls asleep. *Today* Christ is transfigured on Mount Tabor. *Today* the sun is darkened, and the earth quakes, as the Son of God hangs on the Cross.

Today Christ sleeps.

Today:

Christ is risen from the dead, death He has trampled down by death, and to those in the tombs, He has given life.

ALMS

WE MIGHT WELL ASK, again and again, what should we *do* as Christians? Is there any clear directive in the Gospels as to how we should conduct ourselves, for our own edification and that of others? Shall we once again find contradictory directions? Might there be on this level a sure road to satisfying our Master?

What about alms? charity? Surely there can be nothing ambiguous in this field of Christian behaviour?

The first demand where charity is concerned is that of secrecy (*Matthew 6:3ff*): 'But when thou doest alms, let not thy left hand know what thy right hand doeth.' This is akin to fasting rules: that we should not advertise the fact of fasting by any form of lean or hungry look. Such a command seems relatively easy, although it still may be quite pleasant if someone accidentally discovers that we happen to be the generous anonymous donor – it may not be easy to subdue a quick gleam of pleasure.

The promise given to the charitable is certainly encouraging: we can identify ourselves in intention, if not always in practice, with the sheep (*Matthew 25:31ff*). The last collection for earthquake victims was certainly boosted by our offering, Christmas dinners for the homeless were not unsupported, clothing for refugees has been bountifully provided, boxes have rattled for orphan children's homes. Even dogs and horses have not been forgotten, and the stray cat given milk – a charity perhaps not envisaged in the Gospels, but then times change.

Yes, all that can be reasonably demanded of us, we can in all conscience say that we have attempted: fed the hungry, visited the sick, considered prison conditions (if not visited the prisoner), contributed to homes for the homeless, paid taxes for the care of the aged, and the schooling of children. Have we not, in this department of life, earned one way, however narrow, to slip into heaven?

For one glorious moment it might seem that we have found a way for assurance of salvation. And then … 'There came unto him a woman having an alabaster box of very precious ointment, and poured it on his head, as he sat at meat' (*Matthew 26:7ff*). All that precious ointment, all that money which could have fed poor wretches, all those years of careful saving (for was it not an alabaster box?) all gone! In one instant of time, literally poured away.

No wonder the disciples saw it as a rash and stupid act, an improvident impertinence, 'for this ointment might have been sold for much, and given to the poor'. *Given to the poor*: surely one of the keys to salvation. 'In as much as ye have done it unto one of the least of these my brothers. ye have done it unto me …' That is precisely what the woman did. She *did* it unto Him: she bypassed the least of his brothers. Her adoration of God came before, at this moment, her love for her neighbour. One command does not refute nor contradict the other. It is not either/or. It is both. But love for God comes first.

Morality makes us 'good' people but not necessarily good Christians. We can always be moral: 'Ye have the poor always with you.' A philanthropist need not be a Christian: but a Christian, jealously guarding his values, should be a philanthropist.

'For I was an hungred, and you gave me meat: I was thirsty, and ye gave me drink: I was a stranger, and ye took me in.' But, so too, 'Verily I say unto you, Wheresoever this gospel shall be preached in the whole world, there shall also this, that this woman hath done, be told for a memorial of her.'

ANGER

THERE ARE NOT MANY PEOPLE, if any, who can truly say that they have never felt anger.

The form anger takes may differ: rage, roar, weep, sulk, throw things, hit out, or, in the very extreme, kill. Yet, the total absence of even the feeling of anger, without any practical demonstration, would be unusual. Are we therefore on safe ground to condemn anger? If anything could be safe for us to judge, would not the condemnation of anger be justified?

Surely, anger is unchristian? We are commanded to turn the other cheek, that the meek will inherit the earth, and, in *Matthew 5:24*, even more explicitly, that we should not dare to approach the altar, to make an offer of love to God, until we are reconciled with our fellow men.

Yet, even as we may risk breathing a sigh of relief that here is no contradiction which human skill may not unravel, even as we rest on the plain statement: 'Agree with thine adversary quickly' (*Matthew 5:25*) or, even as we realize the full danger of anger as a spiritual guilt so deep that it need not even be put into practice for its culpability – anger in the heart is in effect already murder: as *sin* it need not be fulfilled in practice – even at such a moment of apparent clarity and possibility of judgment comes the contradiction – the inevitable finite doubt: 'But I say unto you, That whosoever is angry with his brother without a cause shall be in danger of the judgment ...' (*Matthew 5:22*).

Without cause: there seems the clue for the possibility of self-righteous evasion. If we have cause, we have evangelical permission for anger. Yet, who are we to define what is cause? Can there be cause sufficient enough between one sinner and another? *Without cause*: Is there a touch of irony here? A touch reminiscent of the command to the group of men who brought the woman, caught in the very act of adultery, for Christ's judgment? And His judgment: 'He that is without sin among you, let him first cast a stone at her' (*John 8:7*). Did they not all slink away shamefaced? Is not this the same permission granted to us for being angry: they, if without sin: we, if we have cause? What can we do but join those men and slink off shamefaced, leaving the one to whom we felt anger facing Christ?

No, 'without cause' far from being a loophole for anger surely pins us down even more firmly to the realization of our own sin. But, once there was a real situation of anger with cause, a situation not to be repeated because on that occasion the anger was divinely pure. Our anger cannot be but defiled. There may well be degrees of defilement but absolute purity is not in our grasp, in no human grasp other than in the one Perfect One.

Christ could be angry – and with just cause. He, Perfect Man and Perfect God, saw the desecration of the Holy Temple of His Father, and with divine wrath He 'cast out all them that sold and bought in the temple, and overthrew the tables of the moneychangers, and the seats of them that sold doves' (*Matthew 21:12*). He could do that, because in only too short a time He would seek death on behalf of those very people that they might have eternal life.

Yes, we may allow ourselves to feel righteous anger towards the dictators, the persecutors, the profiteers of the world – but, would we die for them?

THE APOSTLES

WE ARE SO CONCERNED with numbers.

'How many were there in church today?'

'Thousands and thousands at the last huge evangelical meeting.'

A favourite argument: 'Lots of people don't believe at all.' 'Most people aren't baptized now.'

Or, on the other side: 'We've got the largest number of Christians in the country.'

And so on and so forth. Yet, Christ thought twelve sufficient for His needs, and of these, one would betray Him.

Respect for numbers binds us to this world, enslaves us, robs us of the pure spirit of life. The twelve ordained were to carry Christianity to the ends of the world.

God does not spare those whom He chooses: Elijah found that out centuries earlier. But, only the few are chosen, not because of some divine, cruel pre-election, but because only the few *wish* to be chosen:

divine election is of our choice. Jesus called Peter, Andrew, James and John. Matthew arose and followed Him. Yet, another, unnamed, queried the absolute nature of the call: he wished to bury his father first: a duty. For the elect there is no duty but that of obedience to the call: '… let the dead bury their dead'.

The Apostles: the beloved, the innermost circle. Yet, one would betray Him. Why was Judas allowed into this closely linked group of Master and disciples? We do not know. Perhaps to suggest that in this world evil may not be excluded? Do we need evil that good may come? If no Crucifixion – no Resurrection? Is it the divine blessing on doubt? We do not know why even the Apostles should be tainted by evil; but, because we do not know, we are left with nothing but faith to uphold us.

The Apostles: Judas betrayed, Peter denied, others fled. We can take courage, and even as we stumble again and again, we can remember and, together with Peter, weep bitterly.

BAPTISM

WHY IS BAPTISM essential for a Christian? The answer would appear quite simple, perhaps too simple for the sophisticated.

Jesus insisted on baptism, in the first place, for Himself (*Matthew 3:13*). And, His divinity was confirmed at baptism.

He, Himself baptized, instituted baptism for all who followed Him as Christians. After He rose from the dead, He instructed the Apostles (*Matthew 28:19*) to baptize in the name of the Trinity. *Only* the Apostles – only the priests of His Church.

Yet baptism, throughout the centuries of Christianity, has been considered so essential that the Church has allowed, in instances of extreme isolation or of imminent death, any Christian to perform this fundamental rite.

A Christian to be a Christian must be baptized, as the Master ordered, in the Name of the Trinity. We cannot evade, or should not attempt to evade, so direct a command.

However, it is not for us to judge. God's mercy for those who do not fulfil the command for baptism is another matter. We cannot judge. We can only fulfil His direction as far as lies within our power and no further.

Once baptized, we are Christians for better or for worse. We cannot escape the seal by any human decision.

Henceforward, whatever we do, we do as Christians: and whatsoever we do in His Name, however insignificant the act of charity – a drink of water to a scrap of humanity (*Matthew 10:42*) – 'shall in no wise lose his reward'. Such open acknowledgment of belief in Christ/God in the least of our actions is practical Christianity.

BETRAYAL

INSTANCES OF BETRAYAL are not uniform, nor equally culpable.

When Judas betrayed Christ, he did so deliberately: he was not forced into it by terror: he was neither blackmailed nor bullied. Of his own free will, he sought out those concerned and offered to betray his Master. Even the amount to be paid to him was not excessive. Why did he do it? Jealousy? Cupidity? The desire to curry favour with the 'high-ups'? Perhaps Judas was sufficiently cunning to realize that the game was up anyway, and that he might as well profit by the inevitable.

Whatever the reasoning that lay behind it, the act of betrayal was horrible. There surely were other means of identifying Christ than by kissing him? This was betrayal to the uttermost limit of treachery. No wonder that he was forced to kill himself. A few pieces of silver to weigh against one glance from God Incarnate. Truly it had been better for him had he not been born! (*Matthew 26:24*).

How different Peter's betrayal! Peter, the hot-headed, the rash, the impetuous. Peter, who flung himself into the sea, only to sink. Peter, who with his sword, leaped to his Master's defence. Peter, whom Jesus warned so tenderly, when he boasted that he would never betray his Master, 'Verily I say unto thee, That this night, before the cock crow, thou shalt deny me thrice.' Peter, who did deny Him thrice. And Peter, who wept bitterly. His was not planned betrayal of his Master but the instinctive reaction of self-preservation.

We need not be downhearted if in the heat of terror we should betray our faith in Christ – provided we repent. Our repentance needs to be positive, according to our capacity known only within the secret of the individual heart. It probably will not involve the sacrifice of our lives. It may well involve the sacrifice of pride. Peter – all the disciples – forsook Him and fled. But, later, they faced what we pray we may never need to face.

'Lead us not into temptation.' Our fear is not only that we should betray Him in time of trial, but, even more, that we should fail in the courage needed for subsequent redeeming of the betrayal.

Betrayal can be evil – *is* evil – if it stops there. But, equally, betrayal can turn to glory.

THE BLESSED

WHO ARE the blessed?

Matthew 5:3ff:

The poor in spirit
Those who mourn
The meek
Which do hunger and thirst after righteousness
The merciful
The pure in heart
The peacemakers
Which are persecuted for righteousness' sake
When men shall revile you

The culmination:

Rejoice and be exceeding glad.

The Beatitudes, therefore, at any rate in the first place, were addressed to the inner circle of His disciples: they are far from being generalizations.

In effect, the Beatitudes are essentially particular: a warning to His immediate disciples of their spiritual aim, of inevitable persecution, and a reward not in this world.

We are not His immediate disciples: we need not flatter ourselves that we are capable of attaining to any degree of 'success' in any one of the divine stipulations, but at least we know, if only in theory, where we should attempt to be aiming.

And yet again, in no uncertain terms, we are told that suffering has its appointed place in the history of salvation. The mystery of suffering involves the most delicate balance. There is no specific call to seek pain, and yet pain, of any description, unsought, has a meaning even if we are far from understanding it.

Pain and suffering are as distant from any manifestation of divine punishment, or divine wrath, as our imagination can take us. There is only divine compassion. And the promise for the martyrs: 'Rejoice and be exceeding glad: for great is your reward in heaven.' The continuity of witness: 'for so persecuted they the prophets which were before you'.

It is not for us to take the Beatitudes to ourselves: that would indeed be presumptuous. But we can, in full repentance, stand, as it were, on the touchline of the athletic contest which heralds in our time the cold, passive persecution of growing indifference.

CHILDREN

SICKLY PICTURES of Christ patting children on the head – what can the evangelical justification be, if any?

Children – little children – are small: vulnerable: physically weaker than bigger children and, even more so, than adults. And, in spite of any possible child labour, not as lucratively productive as their elders. In fact, particularly when birth control did not obtain, in strict terms of practical value, they were not worth much.

Hordes of children infested the roads, begging, pilfering, filthy carriers of disease, blind, stomachs distended with hunger – the kinds of children who followed any crowd out of natural curiosity and from the hope of gain.

Matthew 19:14: 'Suffer little children, and forbid them not to come unto me, for of such is the kingdom of heaven. And He laid his hands upon them.' Some were brought to Him by parents or relatives, but there were the others. Not brought to Him, the waifs, yet:

'whosoever shall give to drink unto one of these little ones a cup of cold water only in the name of a disciple, verily I say unto you, he shall in no wise lose his reward'.

The child is wretchedly insignificant and the act of charity so small, but in the Name of Christ it has no human measure. An insignificant, unwanted, infested ragamuffin, but any harm done – (*Matthew 18:6*) – better a death by drowning than the consequent retribution.

The positive evil of murder – of thieving – the negative evil of withholding charity however meagre – a cup of cold water – cannot be excused or mitigated by the insignificance of the victim. And, apart from anything else, water did not just flow from a tap. 'But whoso shall offend one of these little ones …'

Pride? The wretched, starving urchins play their part again: 'Whosoever therefore shall humble himself as this little child, the same is greatest in the kingdom of heaven' (*Matthew 18:4*).

There is no possibility of estimating divine values. Again and again we are debarred from penetrating into the mind of God. And so to the question as to who is the greatest in the kingdom of heaven, comes the answer: 'Except ye be converted, and become as little children, ye shall not enter into the kingdom of heaven' (*Matthew 18:3*).

No, not flaxen-haired cherubs round a beautiful shepherd with a flock of sleek sheep, but the lowest of the low. Such is the kingdom of heaven. Or, not necessarily. We cannot know the passport.

CHRIST

TO DEFINE CHRIST is an impossibility. We speak of 'Perfect God' and 'Perfect Man' and this is the furthest we can hope to achieve in the realm of definition. The 'Perfect Man' we may think that we can comprehend, but, if we stop to consider, even that proves impossible.

How can we grasp perfection with our imperfect minds? We can attempt to do so by negative means: Christ, as Perfect Man, was without any form of sin. And then we can begin to enumerate: without greed, without lust, without envy ... but, however far we go in such enumeration, we cannot go beyond the final point of our own human comprehension.

Or we can try the positive approach: to think of all the virtues, as far as we know them. But there again we are brought up before the blank wall of limitation: our virtues, as we know them, are confined to our human potentiality.

If we are stymied by 'Perfect Man', how much

more by 'Perfect God'! How can we even begin to reach God in order to make the attempt at definition? Thus, we must face the fact that Christ, both as God and as Man, is beyond human definition. We cannot attain a definition of God theologically, only in Faith – Incarnate.

But, as a living Truth, a whole new vista opens. He was on earth, and He taught us, and as far as He limited Himself, thus far we can grasp Him. Ultimately, we can but touch the hem of His garment which He, in His love, extends to us. And His love is not our love. Yet again – incomprehensible.

Agony in Gethsemane. (Matthew 26:36ff)
Perfect Man: or, perhaps in this context, perfect *man*. Christ was a human being. His was real agony before He came to His voluntary, ignominious, violent death on the Cross. As God He chose this criminal execution for himself – this degradation. As man, He was in agony, and obeyed the divine will.

What is the meaning of the duality? Why did He not come down from the Cross? Surely, a blessing on suffering. We do not choose to suffer, we are in agony, but we can somehow be upheld by the divine precedent: suffering has this peculiar blessing of its very own. Arrayed in royal purple, God could have chosen to enter into Jerusalem triumphantly, riding on the ass, as was expected of the Messiah. He chose the Cross.

Suffering, sickness, poverty, misery – we surely must try to relieve those in need and pain, but, witnessing such suffering is not a matter for 'losing our faith'.

God, as man, suffered before us. As Christians we are certainly encouraged, if not ordered, to pray for the relief of suffering, for ourselves as well as for others. Such prayers of desolation have been blessed by God Himself. But, even as He prayed for deliverance, came the words '... not as I will, but as thou wilt ...'. Prayer for release from suffering, for relief, for help, yes. But, judging God by results, no.

'My God, my God, why hast thou forsaken me?' God, as man, suffered the last agony of desolation. Sometimes we say, or are tempted to say, 'There is no God', 'Rubbish, all this belief', 'Look round, see the sickness, the hatred, the cruelty', 'You talk of a God of Love, what does He think He's doing then?' 'God of Love – nice sort of love which allows ...' 'Read the newspapers. Listen to the radio. Watch TV – a merciful God of love – are you joking?'

'Are you joking?' 'My God, my God, why hast thou forsaken me?' That was Christ in His agony, as *Perfect* Man. *Perfect* Man: yet in Him was the doubt. Hence surely doubt is *part* of the perfection: doubt is no alien, outside factor: it is integrated. The desolation of abandonment has been blessed.

We, as human beings, cannot avoid doubt: doubt is no sin, nor does it mean that we are deserted. Far from it: in doubt we are drawn into the divine suffering. But why? Inexplicable. Somewhere, beyond our comprehension, there is a meaning.

We must try not to fall into that very common error of attempting to explain suffering, thereby justifying God as a God benevolent and not cruel – nor punitive – nor simply not there. Any such effort is irrelevant and pointless. Suffering remains a mystery.

'My God, my God, why hast thou forsaken me?' And there is no injunction against experiencing the reality of suffering: there is no forbidding of weeping, of lamenting, mourning, defying, battling. We are told to relieve suffering. And yet ultimately, when all else fails and the suffering, undefeated, stares us in the face, then we remember: '… not as I will, but as thou wilt …'.

CHRISTIANITY

CHRISTIANITY? Not an abstract goodness. Not kindness. Not generosity. Not morality. Not self-denial. Not any of the so-called virtues, yet all of them. How? Not anything for its own sake.

Christianity? The following in the steps of Christ. Morality and virtue and all forms of decent behaviour may ensue but, without Christ as the pivot, as the moving force, not *Christ*-ianity.

Christianity is the goodness, which is not goodness in its own right, but as the overflow from the fountainhead, Christ. Goodness which does not overflow from the fountainhead, Christ, which is unconnected however tenuously with the Divine Centre, is not Christianity.

A non-Christian may have every possible virtue, but he is yet not a Christian. A Christian may have every possible vice, but he is still a Christian, albeit a nasty one!

Christianity, in the one fundamental sense, is a *technical* term for one baptized into Christ.

THE CHURCH

HOW CAN WE AVOID false prophets? How have we
been told to recognize the true Church? To be confident of the validity of those who profess to instruct us
in the truth? Can we ever be *certain*, in human, logical
terms?

The Apostle Thomas was not blamed for his
doubt: he was, as might appear strange, blessed for it. In
the blessing, in the divine positive acceptance of
Thomas's doubt, we discover that we, on our part, need
no longer be afraid of doubt. The doubt is not the
enemy: the doubt may well be our way into His side: the
doubt may well be the positive road to the true Christ.

If we are offered a safe road, comprehensible and
exclusive, then flee temptation. There is no such easy
way. But is there any firm ground? Only one. The living God: the Gospels. And again: Is there any firm
path to the Gospels? To an understanding of their
texts? To this there would appear only the one possible answer: the Church.

So, to the same question: How do we avoid false prophets? Which is *the* Church? Back to the Gospels. *Matthew 7:24*: 'Therefore whosoever heareth these sayings of mine, and doeth them, I will liken him unto a wise man, which built his house upon a rock ...'

So far so good. But where? Who? How do we recognize this rock? *Matthew 16:18*: 'And I say also unto thee, That thou art Peter, and upon this rock I will build my church; and the gates of hell shall not prevail against it.'

Only the Apostles, Peter, James, and John were allowed to witness the Transfiguration. (Who but a priest should enter into the Sanctuary?) Only the chosen eleven were to meet the Risen Christ in Galilee (*Matthew 28:19*). And only they were told to go out into the world, baptizing, and teaching: '... and, lo, I am with you alway, even unto the end of the world.' Amen.

The Church may have divided over the centuries, through envy, pride, lust for power, but however corrupt, however fragmented, there can only be *one* Church, that Church which was founded by Christ God, and descended through the Apostles. However, even here, we can neither judge nor even dare to be blindly exclusive: 'other folds I have'.

St Peter betrayed Christ. St Thomas doubted. St Paul persecuted. What sort of Church is this? *The*

Church is beyond human corruption but the *bishops* and the *priests* are human. This dichotomy we are certainly told to remember: no false idolatry of the man, but due reverence for the office. '… All therefore whatsoever they bid you observe, that observe and do; but do not ye after their works: for they say, and do not' (*Matthew 23:3*).

Something essential to remember, as an integral part of the unbroken line of the episcopate: when the line is broken, then only the man remains and that is indeed a heavy burden for the man and any flock he gathers round him: shut in on themselves, their virtues, their sins, and no open window to a dimension outside of their own making.

Matthew 9:16ff: 'No man putteth a piece of new cloth unto an old garment, for that which is put in to fill it up taketh from the garment, and the rent is made worse …' We do not *continue* from the Old Testament, but we *fulfil* it – quite another matter. Christ fulfilled the Old Testament by every word He spoke: from Law into Spirit. Christianity fulfils Judaism – is neither antagonistic nor corresponding – but it is the Rock established on the soil prepared by the Law and the Prophets.

Matthew 16:23: 'But he turned, and said unto Peter, Get thee behind me, Satan.' Peter – that very hour appointed as the Rock of the Church – is now severely reprimanded for interfering in what he has not as yet grasped: the necessity for his Master to suffer. The Church, founded by God, is still human – as Peter was. Therefore the Church is fallible on the human level. Hence 'Economy': the readiness, if necessary, to deny its own disciplinary rules. But never the Faith.

Matthew 16:19: 'And I will give unto thee the keys of the kingdom of heaven'. Is not this akin to 'strait is the gate, and narrow is the way which leadeth unto life, and few there be that find it' (*Matthew 7:14*)? But, in glorious contradiction: 'But with God all things are possible' (*Matthew 19:26*).

THE COMMANDMENTS

THE COMMANDMENTS of the Old Testament may well be seen as the paradox of the New.

Yes, obviously we must keep the Commandments, and yes, equally obviously, we must not regard them as absolute or as taking priority over the New Testament of Christ. But being Christians does not absolve us from our fundamental obedience.

Christianity transfigures and fulfils the Law but never denies it in its essence. Christianity allows for no idolatry, not even of the Commandments: they must be obeyed in spirit, in practice, but never as a goal or end in themselves. Milestones, yes: destination, no. Hence the parable of the Good Samaritan.

The lawyer's question (*Matthew 22:36*) 'Master, which is the great commandment in the law?' is answered in *Luke 10:25ff*: 'love your neighbour'. The question: who is my neighbour? To follow that path would be to follow the Law, to be the passive recipient of divine ordinance. A tidy situation and attainable: to know precisely how far and to whom our love should extend.

And this is precisely where the Old Law is lifted up from earthly dimensions and fulfilled in the New. Where the faithful Jew merges into the Christian. Love is not a question to be answered by the Law – who is my neighbour? whom am I in duty bound to love? – Love is a question of love: am I he who loves his neighbour? The identity of the neighbour is essential for the fulfilling of the Law. The identity of the neighbour is entirely irrelevant for the fulfilling of the Gospel of Christ – the more unclean the better.

Yet, even here, we are in danger. Again and again we are reined back in our desire for absolute knowledge of the way to salvation. Love our neighbour. Yes. But to love our neighbour still remains the *second* commandment. The first (*Matthew 22:37*) 'Thou shalt love the Lord thy God with all thy heart, and with all thy soul, and with all thy mind.' And only *secondly*, as it were spilling over from the first, 'Thou shalt love thy neighbour as thyself.'

In this divine, clear subordination, we, as Christians, are for ever reminded of our spiritual values. The 'priorities' of humanism and Christianity are mutually exclusive. The practice *alone* of the second Commandment, Christ's directive to love our neighbour, will not *in itself* make us Christians: it might

28

make us nice people, but that is not necessarily the same thing.

Again and again the Gospels face us with this technical aspect of Christianity: not to be confused with fulfilment or otherwise in behaviour. *Sunday Observance*: – so often misidentified with the Sabbath observance of the Law. As always, Christ taught the necessity as His followers of avoiding the idolatry inherent in flat obedience to a Law: and, so too, by means of such obedience, the evasion of personal spiritual burden of responsibility (*Matthew 12:1*). When accused by the Pharisees of breaking the Sabbath, of doing that 'Which is not lawful', His answer: 'I will have mercy, and not sacrifice.' 'The Son of man is Lord even of the Sabbath day.'

Was it not a deliberate lesson against the empty keeping of the Law to heal the man with the withered hand on the Sabbath (*Matthew 12:10*)? When asked if it was lawful to heal, His reply: 'It is lawful to do well on the Sabbath days.' – *to do well*. Perhaps this does not include football and shopping. But Sunday is *not* the Sabbath. Sunday is the Day of Resurrection – a day of joyous thanksgiving. A Pasch every week. A day set apart from all other days – of excitement – of gratitude – of awe – as Sunday after Sunday, sinners as we are, yet we are permitted to join those chosen women 'very early in the morning'. There is no Law, but it is a pity to waste a Sunday on ordinary pursuits – but that is a matter for every Christian to decide for himself.

Christ plucked the ears of corn (*Matthew 12:1*) on the Sabbath – He and His disciples were hungry. We go round with our trolley. It is not for us to judge each other: 'The Son of man is Lord even of the Sabbath day.' Whatever else, the Law is not supreme, not even on the Sabbath. And Sunday is not the Sabbath.

THE CROSS

THE GREATEST CONTRADICTION of the Christian faith: God on the Cross. And not even a magnificent, specially designed Cross, but one of many – squat in shape – death rows for the lowest criminals.

Matthew 16:24: Jesus to His disciples: 'If any man will come after me, let him deny himself, and take up his cross, and follow me.'

Three stages: first, the willed intention to follow Christ – an effort of the mind – a decision. Neither sentimental nor passive – not in the least emotional or excited – not under any outside dramatic influence. 'If any man will come after me …': the objectivity of the decision surely cannot be overemphasized. And an act where no return is envisaged: 'let him deny himself' – forget one's comfort, pleasure, needs, forget one's preferences in any sphere, forget *oneself* – that part which cries out to be satisfied on whatever level.

'… and take up his cross': of one's own will accept all the suffering which may beset us, through our own intemperance, or illness, or assaults from outside, but, primarily, assaults from within. One aspect of our cross, unlike that of Christ, is ever entwined with our tendency to sin – the evil within. And this we must face, openly confess it, and turn it to good.

'and follow me'. We cannot follow Christ to His Crucifixion, His Resurrection, until we have faced our own crosses and from the negative evil of sin turned them into positive work of repentance: picked them up unflinchingly and thereby become as ready as we can ever be to follow Christ. Bluntly, we must crucify ourselves before we can begin to live. Then only, somehow, stumbling under the weight of sin, dead but alive, we follow to the Resurrection.

'For whosoever will save his life shall lose it: and whosoever will lose his life for my sake shall find it' (*Matthew 16:25*). And we must not forget 'for my sake'. There is, as ever, the sharp dividing line which is not to be ignored: anybody can be 'good', that is not the point. There is also God's embracing love which knows no human limitation. It is not for us to judge. But a Christian is marked out, however poor a person he may be, by the words of identification: 'for my sake'.

The promise is great but so too the responsibility. *For Christ's sake*: not for motives of kindness, not for moral promptings of the conscience, not for social awareness. Not ethical. All of these, on one level, but apparently pointless as the work of the spirit if not for *Christ's* sake. If we are Christians.

DEATH

Matthew 27:50: 'Jesus, when he had cried again with a loud voice, yielded up the ghost.'

The death on the Cross was real. Sometimes, its reality verges on taking second place to the glory of the Resurrection – the reality of the human suffering on the Cross, the pain, the desolation.

God Incarnate died on the Cross. Thereby the greatest fear of humanity – death – is divinely blessed. God *chose* death as the means of salvation. From a human point of view He need not have done so. But He did. Without the death of God Incarnate, death for man would not have been trodden down. Death He overcame by death, for He resurrected. Death has no more dominion over man. For God was true man, even as He was true God.

Christ's Resurrection was in the body. Thomas was allowed to establish the reality of the risen body. Death takes on a peculiar magnificence of its own: the medium of life.

DIVINE AUTHORITY

ONCE AGAIN we come up short with the limitations of our human minds.

Intellectual pride, even in the guise of seeking the truth, will get us nowhere beyond the blank wall of created confinement: so much to do within the enclosure, why beat our heads against the radiance of the Unattainable?

Matthew 21:23ff: The arrogant question put to the Incarnate God: 'By what authority doest thou these things? and who gave thee this authority?' A question, in various forms, which has occupied the minds of theologians for centuries. But God is not to be questioned in human terms.

A delicate and conclusive twist to the answer. The answer is a question. Question for question: 'The baptism of John, whence was it? From heaven, or of men?' The questioners were in a quandary, afraid to deny John the Baptist's validity, for they feared the people. Hence prevarication: 'We cannot tell'.

And the answer, so divinely simple, so devastating to human pride: 'Neither tell I you by what authority I do these things.'

They *cannot*. He *will* not.

It is surely no accident that this contemporary assault of speculative theology is confronted forthwith with the disturbing picture of publicans and harlots who 'go into the kingdom of God' before those who question in all righteousness the validity of the absolute, incomprehensible Divine Authority.

DIVINE JUDGMENT

Matthew 13:24ff: '… The kingdom of heaven is likened unto a man which sowed good seed in his field.'

In God there is no evil: He is *the* Good. He is *the* Love. His creation is good: His creatures are good. But there is evil. The evil from the Evil One. The Enemy. And we have free will, the choice.

The seed sown by the Enemy, the tares, the weeds which try to choke the wheat, need not be allowed to grow. Nor need the good seed be choked. It may seem inevitable. God will not interfere, nor will He allow His servants to interfere: 'lest while ye gather up the tares, ye root up also the wheat with them'.

Once again the divine warning against any presumption of judgment. Not even the intimate, faithful servants are allowed to judge. No human creature may judge a fellow human creature. No human being may interpret for God. Tares and wheat must grow together.

In this world sin is inescapable. Evil cannot be excluded. In *this* world. But there will be a Day of Judgment. A Day, whatever form it takes, when God will divide the tares from the wheat, the sheep from the goats, the barren tree from the fruitful. Only God knows the day, only God knows the judgment.

But one thing we *can* know – we *can* know that we do *not* know the tares from the wheat in heavenly terms.

There will be surprises. 'When saw we thee sick, or in prison, and came unto thee?' And, in the opposite direction: 'When saw we thee an hungred, or athirst, or a stranger, or naked, or sick, or in prison, and did not minister unto thee?'

The sheep and the goats: divine judgment beyond comprehension in life or in death. We can only beg for mercy again and again. We can only pray as we stumble in the darkness of ignorance, distraught by doubt, yet the doubt urging us on to the unattainable goal of solution. We can only rejoice in our agony that God's judgment is not ours: 'Let both grow together until the harvest.'

And after the harvest? The longed-for security: 'gather the wheat into my barn'. The *peace* of heaven – and the *work* in heaven: wheat does not lie unused.

Matthew 7:1: 'Judge not, that ye be not judged.'

What is judgment? Does it mean that we should

not try to discriminate between good and bad as we perceive them? That we must accept malice, thieving, rape, murder, as something inevitable? That we smooth over evil action with psychological terms or sentimental excuses? That there is no moral code whatsoever? No responsibility for our families – as long as they are so-called happy? Does it mean that as Christians we must countenance every sacrilege?

The word is *judge*. There is only one *Judge*. So back to the fundamental delusion of Satan: that we can be as God. The tree of knowledge. *Judge not.* Seek not to enter into the mind of God. Quite a different matter from acting within our own limitations.

Do not say who will go to hell, who to heaven. We do not know. Do not say, 'You have offended God.' We do not know. Do not speak as from God. Condemn, if we must condemn, out of human weakness, not in the presumption of divine approval.

In this world we surely must at times contend with evil on many levels, but contend in repentance, not in assertion of divine right. We fight because we must not judge. No human principle is absolute. Christians we are, we pray that we are not *of* the world, but we remain *in* the world.

Matthew 20:16: 'So the last shall be first, and the first last.' Divine justice, wholly unlike human, above all is not relative. Each one of us, sheep or goat, is *one*

– on every level individual. God sees us as individual.

This world is finite, hence every part is identified relatively: black is black vis-à-vis white. We know industry through idleness. So we come to the vineyard and the blinding revelation of the Absolute Divine. Divine judgment is not relative. Hence, for us, it is incomprehensible. We would expect the labourers in the vineyard to be paid according to the hours which they had worked. To be rewarded relatively to their labour: one hour – three – six – nine. And the eleventh hour. But the reward for each was identical.

Relatively, the reward was unjust. If the workers in the vineyard had been able to judge absolutely, then what the next man received in payment would have been totally irrelevant. We cannot avoid thinking relatively, for we are human, but there is no necessity to judge, for such judgment cannot avoid being relative and wholly uncomprehending the judgment of God.

Our work: austerely to refrain from looking sideways. To accept gladly 'I do thee no wrong.' Divine justice is not ours. Ours is not His.

DIVINE PROVIDENCE

LET US LOOK at the constant repetitive *why* – starting, as it were, from the very beginning.

Why the Jews? *Why* Mary of all the Jewish virgins? *Why* that particular time? *Why* the eleven faithful Apostles and not anyone else? *Why* Judas to betray – there were no doubt many others who might have done it more wholeheartedly. So many an incomprehensible *why*.

And how can we judge the importance of why that particular man, nameless, was chosen for the use of his upper room for the keeping of the Passover? Or, again, a really puzzling question: why was Pilate's wife troubled by a dream? Nothing, apparently, came of that dream other than Pilate's not listening to its warning. So, it would be impossible, and useless on every level, to search the Scriptures for the answer to Divine Providence – the answer, at least, on human, logical terms.

All we can begin to understand is that Divine

Providence is the highest mystery, yet in no way an imposition on our human spiritual, moral, physical freedom. Mary need not have accepted the agonizing grace proffered to her. Andrew need not have followed the first call, nor fetched his brother. The nameless man could have refused the use of his upper room. Pilate might have heeded his wife's warning. No-one forced Judas to betray his Master with a kiss.

There emerges an infinity of difference in Divine Providence: divine foreknowledge and divine predestination. We are free – terrifyingly free – to betray God. But God can weep. And tenderly God says to him on whom He built His Church – sad paradox – '… this night, before the cock crow, thou shalt deny me thrice.' Jesus wept.

DIVINE VALUE

WHAT IS BIG? What small? What rich? What poor? What are numbers in any evangelical connotation? In effect, what do we, or what can we, understand of the worth, if any, in God's eyes of our human so-called spiritual achievements?

Matthew 13:3ff: the parable of the sower. God's prodigality in our estimation: the sower seemed to sow without any consideration for the condition of the land. He broadcast His seed indiscriminately into good, bad, shallow, infected, rich soil. He did not stint His seed and the seed, as it were, once sown, became autonomous: some grew, some yielded to outward pressure at various stages of growth, some never began. No value seemed to be put on the cost of the seed and its potential profit.

Divine prodigality – the generosity of divine love – and so too our incapability even to begin to measure the scope of divine love: we cannot see into God's values. There is no explicit grading of the good seed –

some seed managed to multiply a hundredfold, some sixty, some thirty: and there is no hint as to the importance laid on the comparative fertility.

This is very much as in the parable of the vineyard: we cannot judge the value of the work done in the eleventh hour. Moreover, it is not our business to judge the efficacy of the seed as it is not our business to judge in the vineyard (*Matthew 20:1ff*).

In our earthly realm all is relative: in the divine, all is absolute in the sense that every human creature is judged entirely by himself – not in comparison with any other human creature. It is surely part of our work on earth to learn only to look at ourselves, close scrutiny of our own activity irrespective of our neighbour. It is certainly not our business to embark on the impossible ploy of estimating our neighbour's spiritual achievement.

Again and again we come up against the same demand, whatever the context: judge not. Seek not to judge man or God. Nothing will enable us to see into the heart of man – or into the mind of God.

After the difficulties experienced by the rich young man, the warning follows that it is easier for a camel to get through a needle's eye than for a rich man to find a way into heaven. And yet, 'with God all things are possible'. Even those, however, who have given up everything, or believe that they have, may have a shock. Who can dare to be certain that he has given up *everything*? Can 'everything' be identical for each individual soul? 'Many that are first shall be last and the last shall be first' (*Matthew 19:30*).

Our work: to work blindly, in faith. Never to rely on any 'achievement'. Yet, ever to be assured, and reassured, of the prodigality of God's love, and of His inscrutable evaluation of His creation.

EVANGELICISM

WE ARE NOT ALL chosen to spread the Gospel.

Christ gave His explicit instructions only to the chosen disciples and thereby not only did He limit the number who should teach, but He limited also those who should be taught.

The disciples were to confine their work in the first place only to their fellow Jews: 'But go rather to the lost sheep of the House of Israel' (*Matthew 10:6*). To the Jews – their own people – themselves.

The spreading of Christianity is not a business proposition on a worldwide supermarket scale: it is a limited concern with all the inherent dangers of a small and poor business, possibly no immediate material capital available: 'Be ye therefore wise as serpents, and harmless as doves.'

Evangelicism goes with persecution: not with cheering crowds, dancing and clapping, carried away by every emotion unconnected with persecuted isolation. Evangelicism has no fixed programme of self-defence: certainly we must know what we are teaching, if we are called to teach, but we need not prepare equally for any contingency of hostile assault 'for it shall be given you in that same hour what you shall speak'.

Evangelicism does not mean a self-willed surrender to persecution: 'But when they persecute you in this city, flee ye into another …' (*Matthew 10:23*).

Evangelicism does not mean a banging on people's doors when the inhabitants are positively uninterested: Christianity is not a salesman's wares which he is determined to sell whatever the sentiments of his potential customer. The disciple of Christ was not told to insert his foot in order to keep the door open while he thrust his mission down a reluctant throat. Quite the reverse: 'And whosoever shall not receive you, nor hear your words, when ye depart out of that house or city, shake off the dust of your feet.'

We are not told to preach the Gospel of our own will: the harvest may be plenteous, the labourers may be few, but we are told explicitly (*Matthew 9:38*) 'Pray ye therefore the Lord of the harvest, that he will send forth labourers into his harvest.' Not our choice, but His.

And, ever again, what are numbers? Where lies the triumph of a packed church when 'where two or three are gathered together in my name, there am I in the midst of them' (*Matthew 18:20*)? However many, however few, would seem irrelevant compared with the joy of union: 'He that receiveth you receiveth me, and he that receiveth me receiveth him that sent me' (*Matthew 10:40*).

EVIL/SIN

ONE CLUE IN JUDAS: he betrayed Christ. But the betrayal is a confession of faith. If He were not God, why fear and destroy Him? Evil, Sin, Faith somehow are irrevocably connected. If no doubt, no faith: if no evil, no confession of good.

Matthew 13:30 suggests the same: wheat and tares. Wheat, good seed. Tares, sown by the enemy. But the obvious, facile solution of rooting up the tares is not the divine answer. Back to the dialectic of the finite world, the inevitability of the yes/no: nothing absolute. The tares may not go until the Day of Judgment for in the human creature it is not possible neatly to divide the bad from the good. We cannot be perfect.

The 'Resist not evil' (*Matthew 5:39ff*) is not only a Christian directive to suffer beyond the demand, however unjustifiable. But it suggests a voluntary acceptance and performance of the unavoidable: a positive working with the fact that evil in this world is

49

inescapable. So make it our own by a spiritual somersault and transfigure its alien stranglehold.

Yes, sin is unavoidable. Yet we are not necessarily passive. Offences will come. But 'Woe to that man by whom the offence cometh!' There is no possibility of passivity in the life of a Christian. We are not predestined to sin. Sin is there. It remains for us, each according to his capability, to prick the vainglorious balloon: to reduce sin to its shrivelled nonentity by the active strength of love.

We are not to resist evil – not to react and, by reaction, assume the grotesque caricature of the divine intention in His creation.

Matthew 18:7: Offences *will* come. But the first effort should not be the attempt to deal with the evil *outside* but rather with the enemy from *within*. If *our* eyes are evil, how can we think of discerning the evil in others? Or, for that matter, the good?

Our work: repentance. Leave the others to God. Christ seeks the lost sheep (*Matthew 18:12*). Christ calls sinners to repentance (*Matthew 9:13*).

FAITH/DOUBT

Matthew 14:28: The disciples saw Jesus walking on the sea towards their boat and they were afraid. But Peter cried out, 'Lord, if it be thou, bid me come unto thee on the water.'

Inherent trust: faith in the power of Christ to enable him to do the impossible. But, was there a flaw in the faith? Was there lurking somewhere the need to prove, in human terms, Christ's divine authenticity?

'*If* it be thou …' Christ said, 'Come.' Did Peter sink simply because the waves were too great for him, or because he did not wholly believe that it could be God who called him? Yet, even as he began to sink, his cry was 'Lord, save me.' And immediately Jesus did bring him to safety, with the reproach 'O thou of little faith, wherefore didst thou doubt?'

Where was the doubt? Not in God's power, but, rather, in God's presence. The doubt opposed the faith: the *fact* was there, there was the actuality of Christ's invitation, but the faith wavered.

What could be a more striking example than this that faith and doubt are inseparable: not faith and fact – the fact of Christ was there – but faith failed to sustain the doubt in His divine power.

Doubt was only once to be magnificently settled by fact. Thomas was invited to put his hand into the crucified side: otherwise, even during His time in the world, Christ demanded faith from those who followed Him: the living ever with the doubt.

Matthew 15:22ff: The faith of the Canaanite woman: daring faith and love.

Such was the woman's love for her daughter but even greater her faith in Christ's power to heal and His generosity. Faith gave her wisdom: faith taught her that there is no boundary to love – the children's bread of love is inexhaustible – there are always the crumbs.

And her faith taught her that seeking God's love cannot be a passive occupation. Some effort of faith must be made: even the effort of licking up the crumbs.

Faith teaches to wait hungrily – hopefully – and never to be ashamed or afraid to beg for what is needed: 'And her daughter was made whole from that very hour.'

Matthew 16:6ff: Once again, faith is set directly antithetical to doubt.

The disciples are rebuked for thinking that Jesus

was speaking of the reality of actual bread: their faith was lacking because they had not understood that He spoke, in image, of the error, the 'leaven' in the teaching of the Pharisees and Sadducees. The disciples had not grasped Christ's warning against the false assurance of salvation preached by the Pharisees and the Sadducees: their bread might rise, but it was not the real, the true bread.

The work of faith is to learn how to discern between the true and the false. Christ alone is the true Bread of Life. Hence the rebuke to His disciples: their blindness in discerning the false from the true. Knowledge was not at issue. Only faith.

FAMILY

HERE WE MEET resolved contradiction at its sharpest.

The Commandments must be kept: we must honour fathers and mothers: of this there is no question. But, equally, there is no question, *Matthew 19:29*: 'And everyone that hath forsaken houses, or brethren, or sisters, or fathers, or mothers ... shall receive a hundredfold and shall inherit everlasting life.'

Does the answer not lie, if answer there is, in the very fact of the precious sanctity of the family? If family ties were not as sacred, then the act of breaking them would have by far the less significance.

The demand to follow Christ could not have been put more forcefully: where lies the urgency or paramount importance in leaving something of little worth?

Once again, the First and Second Commandments are brought into sharp relief: not *contradicting* each other but enhancing the importance of each.

Bluntly: if our family were of no worth, there

would be no suggestion of risk, nor of sacrifice, in the forsaking both of natural affection, and, perhaps even more, the safety of the clan.

And there would be no overt, no positive acceptance of the two great Commandments – in their *correct*, divinely ordained order.

FASTING (FOOD REGULATIONS)

NOW, WE CAN REALLY have fun as practising Orthodox Christians: we are free to scoff at the Catholics who are not keeping up to our standards, we can pity the poor Protestants who know nothing of liturgical fasting, and we can occupy ourselves during the Great Lent in working out delicious recipes which are 'quite alright, all the correct ingredients'.

Ultimately, God alone will judge. Which is breaking the spirit of the law? Not to fast? Or to spend hours and money on keeping to special food, once easily obtainable in Greece or Russia, but foreign luxuries for us? What do we do? What can we do?

Matthew 4:2: Jesus fasted forty days and forty nights in the wilderness.

Matthew 15:11: 'Not that which goeth into the mouth defileth a man; but that which cometh out of the mouth, this defileth a man.'

Very important: lack of ostentation in fasting, either in appearance, or, possibly, more appropriate to our times, in the exchange of recipes: when you fast, fast inconspicuously: 'anoint thy head and wash thy face ...' (*Matthew 6:16ff*).

Fasting has been ordained for us. No fasting while the Bridegroom is with us (*Matthew 9:15*), no fasting by arbitrary timing of one's own, sno fasting beyond the ordinances of the Church: avoid the temptation of self-willed righteousness, of the spiritual arrogance which goes beyond the limitations laid down by the Church.

Yet, equally, no escape from 'but the days will come, when the bridegroom shall be taken from them, and then shall they fast' (*Matthew 9:15*).

Why do we fast? Because Christ said that we should. But *how* we approach fasting is a matter for some consideration. Nowhere is it suggested that we should choose our own methods.

FORGIVENESS

FORGIVENESS IS A MYSTERY. When do we really forgive as opposed to a formal, cerebral motion of forgiving?

Forgiveness is not passive: it is not a question of not seeking revenge: it is not a question of not harbouring feelings of active resentment: it is, in fact, never a 'not'. We are carefully led from the recognizing of palpable lack of forgiveness to the true forgiveness which far surpasses the demands of moral decency.

Most of us can, more or less, manage the first stage of the work of forgiveness. 'Then came Peter to him and said, Lord, how oft shall my brother sin against me, and I forgive him? till seven times?' Seven times: what more can we do? But do we stop abruptly at the expiration of the stipulated time? Is it still a question of law? Is forgiveness a cold, objective, circumscribed, intellectual gesture?

Immediately Peter is reproached for allocating

forgiveness to a legal behaviour pattern: 'I say not unto thee, Until seven times: but, until seventy times seven.'

Forgiveness is of the Spirit not of the Law. Forthwith, we are brought face to face with the shame of an unforgiving heart: of calculated charity. The King forgave the servant, so heavily in debt. 'But the same servant went out, and found one of his fellow servants, which owed him an hundred pence' … the debt was much less: how could it not be? One servant to another. Yet, such is the innate meanness, we can hardly wait to exact debts from each other. It is not even a practical question: even though we may bring ourselves, on the practical level, to forgive some offence, that is not sufficient: such forgiveness is merely on the moral level. We are told explicitly that we must forgive *from our hearts*. And only each one of us can know what that means for ourselves: there is no all-embracing umbrella rule.

A frightening thought: we might appear to forgive; not exact vengeance; not seek to punish; not and not. But the forgiveness must be from the heart – the last innermost core of self-love. Only then 'So likewise shall my heavenly Father do also unto you'. So also will we be liable to eternal punishment 'if ye from your hearts forgive not every one his brother their trespasses'. *From the heart*. No outside criterion of forgiveness: human or Divine.

FREE WILL

THERE IS SOMETIMES in our minds confusion between divine predestination and divine foreknowledge: the two are far from one.

Predestination would appear to be the final contradiction of the individual freedom to work towards what we understand as salvation or damnation. The belief in predestination, in effect, however much we may wriggle and split terms, would yet seem to mean that whatever we do, including the wriggling, is predestined: each one of us is predestined to heaven or hell.

The concept of predestination, at its basis, may not demand individual passivity, for activity may be the predestined lot of that particular soul, but, however we approach it, any belief in predestination must surely rob us, in practice, of the spiritual incentive towards good or evil.

There is a world of difference between divine predestination and divine foreknowledge. Divine predestination somehow suggests even a cruel God who has chosen, in some arbitrary fashion, some of us to be saved, and others to be damned. And that simply does not make sense with that same God Incarnate dying on the Cross for our salvation! The ways of God are inscrutable but they are not senseless.

God is love. Is love likely to damn some of those He has created, from the moment of their birth, if not earlier? What for? But that does not mean that God is not all-knowing.

Christ knew that Judas would betray him – but He did not pre-elect him to do so. The evil is in us, subject to our control. There is no evading personal guilt by the plea of predestination, the transferring of our guilt upon our Creator.

To betray his Master was the sole decision of Judas: Judas *chose* to do so: God knew that he would do so. But it remained Judas's personal choice – and Judas's personal guilt – '... woe unto that man by whom the Son of man is betrayed'.

HOLY COMMUNION

Matthew 26:26–28: 'And as they were eating, Jesus took bread, and blessed it, and brake it, and gave it to the disciples, and said, Take, eat; this is my body. And he took the cup, and gave thanks, and gave it to them, saying, Drink ye all of it; For this is my blood of the new testament, which is shed for many for the remission of sins.'

Suppose there were no theologians – no hundreds and hundreds of years of discussion and counterdiscussion and doctrine evolved and preached: doctrine against doctrine even to persecution and death in the name of Christ. Suppose, as for the very first time, we read these words, as a child might do – no preconceived ideas, no theological axes to grind. It could be indeed a personal revelation not only of the awesome, inscrutable, incomprehensible nature of God – of His condescension – but also of something of what was divinely ordained for our subsequent attitude, to this very day, towards the Divine Liturgy.

Christ certainly neither despised nor neglected women. He loved them, the bad and the good. And God chose for the Son to have a human mother. The women did not feel rejected – far from it. They followed Christ. They were chosen to witness to His Resurrection. Yet, in the institution of the Sacrament of Holy Communion, the women were not included.

Christ entrusted His Body and His Blood to His chosen Apostles. Surely it is for their ordained successors, and for no-one else, to give us to eat and to drink.

THE HOLY SPIRIT

LET US CONSIDER the Third Person of the Holy Trinity:

'... All manner of sin and blasphemy shall be forgiven unto men: but the blasphemy against the Holy Ghost shall not be forgiven unto men. And whosoever speaketh a word against the Son of man, it shall be forgiven him: but whosoever speaketh against the Holy Ghost, it shall not be forgiven him, neither in this world, neither in the world to come' (*Matthew 12:31–2*).

Terrifying, explicit words: the unforgivable sin – denial of Christ's divinity – the ultimate blasphemy of refusing to confess Christ, perfect God. Christ: the second Person of the Trinity.

The unforgivable sin: denial of the parity – Orthodox dread of any suggestion of the blasphemy against the Holy Spirit – hence the bitter battle of the *filioque*: the merest possibility of misinterpretation of the Creed. Guard the divinity of the Perfect Man whatever the cost.

'He that is not with me is against me' (*Matthew 12:30*) – a demand for the positive affirmation of Christ's divinity: of the presence of the Holy Spirit. But how is it possible for us, sinners that we are, to recognize Christ God? How not be against Him? Only through the work of the Holy Spirit in us: no wonder we pray again and again the prayer of the Trinity, with the final plea to the Spirit: 'O Holy One visit and heal our infirmities for your name's sake.'

And, yet, Christ does not abandon us to this terrifying, absolute dictum of 'He that is not with me is against me.' Even as we settle comfortably into a righteous heretic-hunting mood comes the reminder that it is not for us to judge. We are brought up sharply. We cannot know the dividing line (*Mark 9:40*) 'For he that is not against us is on our part.'

There are no chosen people for Christ, our God. Not by any widest form of preselection, predestination. Each of us, baptized in the Holy Spirit, whoever we have been, is now *personally* responsible for his thoughts, words, deeds. '… but the blasphemy against the Holy Ghost shall not be forgiven unto men.'

What can we do even at the eleventh hour? The Church is built on the deepest human foundation: repentance.

JEWS

THE FIRST CHRISTIANS, Christ's mother, Joseph, the bridegroom, the Apostles – they were all Jews. What is meant therefore in the Gospels in the references to the Jews, frequently in derogatory terms?

It does seem that, by the Jews, in certain contexts, is meant specifically those Jews who would not acknowledge Him: who kept zealously to the Law, either through conviction or through fear, or, yet again, indifference: 'Therefore say I unto you, the kingdom of God shall be taken from you, and given to a nation bringing forth the fruits thereof' (*Matthew 21:43*).

In that sense, in our unbelief, our cowardice, our indifference, we are the Jews. Even as they had the Law to which they clung so tenaciously, which seemed to them like some essential lifeline, we have our laws – our social services – our nondiscrimination – our politically correct – our equal rights – and our fascism and our communism – and our arrogance: our denial that in the beginning He made them male and female.

Surely, therefore, the threat hangs over us: the Kingdom of God shall be taken from us. How long will He suffer our patronizing attitude? We do not even persecute Him. We merely merge Him with false gods lest we should offend each other.

THE KINGDOM OF HEAVEN

ONE ASPECT STANDS OUT very clearly: the *exclusive* nature of the Kingdom of Heaven. The qualifications for entry are not for human understanding but they certainly do not suggest that the first on earth will be amongst the first to enter: shocks there will be.

Matthew 13:31ff: The mustard seed – the most inconspicuous of seeds – but what happens? It becomes a mighty tree. One instance of our not anticipating humanly logical values for the Kingdom of Heaven or, indeed, for entry. Divine love is not sentimental.

Matthew 13:33: The Kingdom of Heaven works secretly and in its ineffable mystery, it is not some-*where* – a distant place – it is of course beyond all human concept of limitation of time and space: it can be, as it were, in 'heaven', but equally it is within ourselves – working within us – making us grow according to divine measure.

Again and again comes the suggestion of secrecy

– of isolation from most of the world – and, above all, the few in number who search for and recognize the Kingdom and its inestimable value: the treasure *hidden* in the field, found only by the one man (*Matthew 13:44*); the *one* pearl which the merchant recognized for its worth, and disposed of the others (*Matthew 13:46*). All the others had to go, because the Kingdom of Heaven demands total dedication, the poverty of leaving father, mother, family, all the goodly pearls of the world – and they *are* goodly.

There was nothing wrong with the other pearls, but if the one is discovered, the others need to lose all significance. Again, the fish was *sorted* (*Matthew 13:48*). This is like the story of the sower: He sowed with divine prodigality – broadcast – and the good seed was negligible in number. The bad fish, caught in the same net as the good, were cast out – *cast out*.

In various images the warning comes repeatedly: the door is shut. The bridegroom is within. The Kingdom of Heaven is everywhere yet terrifyingly exclusive. Cast out. Shut out. Thrown on the fire. Always the apparently impossible demand as the passport for entry.

The marriage of the king's son (*Matthew 22:1ff*): The invited guests found lawful reasons for not attending, yet the man who was therefore compelled to come in was cast out into outer darkness, a wretched evildoer, for not wearing a wedding garment: totally unjust we might say. We can guess at all sorts of answers for this apparently cruel treatment. But the best, surely, might well be that we do not know the answer.

The Kingdom of Heaven – a mystery. There can be no comparison with human judgment: we judge by practical circumstances, how else? The Kingdom of Heaven judges by standards whose measures are unattainable by the human mind. And the judgment would appear so often to be connected with the intention, rather than the achievement. We can only surmise, somewhat vaguely, that the man without the wedding garment should have had the garment if his heart – his mind – were in some way obedient to the divine command. The invitation to the wedding feast? The call of love? Ignored – or inadequately answered? He answered presumptuously: his *own* clothes. At least the invited guests did not come at all.

The Kingdom of Heaven (*Matthew 25:1ff*): the ten virgins. Again, the demand that their lamps should be burning. And the ruthless exclusion of the five foolish ones. Again, the door was shut. But, the thief was allowed in. Perhaps they did not repent but merely lamented their exclusion: perhaps they thought that putting things right on the worldly level would allow for their entrance. When they came back with the oil, they only asked to be let in, there was no word of remorse. How can we know? How can we judge them? But the door was shut.

The Kingdom of Heaven (*Matthew 25:14ff*): the parable of the talents. Yet again, the demand for faith – the apparent distance of the Kingdom of Heaven in time and in space – for the master of the servants was travelling away into a far country: so far, that we can hardly remember the necessity for serving Him that we might enter His Kingdom. The vital importance of working while He is not with us: once again, the inscrutable nature of qualifying for entry into the Kingdom: what were these talents which He entrusted to His servants? And no excuses possible. The fear of God is certainly not a qualification for entry if such fear leads to atrophy. Fear must be one with love, not opposed to it. And love means work, in blind faith. Active fear/love: such is the paucity, and the wealth, of the hints of salvation: the mystery of salvation.

We are left with the child, of no apparent significance in the world – weak – dependent. We are left with the tiny seed, the particle of leaven. *Matthew 18:3*: 'Except ye be converted, and become as little children, ye shall not enter into the kingdom of heaven.'

THE LAW

THE ESSENTIAL DIVISION between the Old and the New: the division, and, paradoxically, the fulfilment.

What seems to us, and to the Jews of His time, a denial of the Law, God, in His love, love which does not exclude, taught as the perfecting of the Law: the taking from the letter into the spirit. To obey a law, even a law honoured as a divine ordinance, as the law, and not as its purpose, was and remains idolatry.

The Law teaches us morality – behaviour – what is due to God and our fellow men. But the Law is not God. The Law may guide, but it must not rule. Exceptions to keeping the Law should be possible. The Law is our servant, to help us to keep on the rails of everyday experience, but the Law is not our master.

When Christ came to fulfil the Law, it did not mean that He came to give it a yet more sovereign place. He came to transfigure it, to reveal the divine spirit, the spirit of the Law, no longer the letter.

The paradox: The Law must be kept – and the

Law must be ignored. We cannot ever be *certain* when to keep and when to ignore. We will fail – and repent. But Christ knew. And He not only taught how sometimes the Law must be set aside, but also how it must be taken further. It works both ways. If we see the Law as somewhere in the middle, then sometimes we must take it further, and at other times obey it less. That is the work of the spirit and the Christian ordeal of not knowing: hence, repentance.

Matthew 5:27ff:
Law: *Sin of adultery.*
Christ: *Sin of adultery in the mind.*
Law: *Permission for divorce.*
Christ: *Only for adultery.*
Law: *An oath must not be broken.*
Christ: *There should be no oath.*
Law: *Eye for eye. Tooth for tooth.*
Christ: *Resist not evil.*
Law: *Law-suit: verdict to take away one's coat.*
Christ: *Give your cloak also.*
Law: *Go a mile, legal distance required.*
Christ: *Go twice the distance legally demanded.*

And, above all else:
Law: *Love your neighbour. Hate your enemy.*
Christ: *Love your enemies, bless them that curse you, do*

good to them that hate you ... Be ye therefore
perfect, even as your Father which is in heaven
is perfect.

For God, in His generous love, sends down His rain
on the just and the unjust.

In effect: each order of Christ's becomes more and
more impossible to attain in practice: they are extrav-
agant demands, the image of the unreachable perfection of the true Christian. None of them should be
taken in isolation from the whole picture of our inadequacy: it is hardly appropriate to stand up in an English court of law and refuse to take the oath! That is
simply not rendering to Caesar what is due to him.
And completely out of the context of impossible aims
set before the Christian.

Never the letter of the Law: never, just one clause,
isolated and made absolute. The Pharisees were horri-
fied that the disciples did not go through the motions
of ritual washing before eating: again, a deliberate
omission for the opportunity to emphasize the importance of what comes *out* of a man's mouth defiling him,
not what goes in or how it goes (*Matthew 15:1ff*).
Again, the living spirit of man, for good or for evil.

And yet Christ never denied the Law – in its right
place – in its structural importance. We need it, as the
wall of the sheepfold, the floor and the roof of the

Upper Room. 'Economy' is no excuse for self-indulgence (*Matthew 26:17ff*). Christ kept the Passover – and all that it entailed. And His entry into Jerusalem (*Matthew 21:1ff*) was such 'that it might be fulfilled which was spoken by the prophet'.

MARRIAGE

IT IS TRUE that we think in contraries, but it is a somewhat horrifying sign of the times that on hearing the word 'marriage' in a Christian context, the immediate reaction so often is a debate on divorce. We seldom stop to think of marriage positively and independently: it always seems to come into some sort of relativity. Marriage for life? Marriage vis-à-vis monasticism? Marriage between faiths? Marriage problems? Interracial marriage? And so forth. But what does the Gospel say of marriage *as* marriage? – as a human bond?

Matthew 19:4–6 seems incontrovertible. 'Have ye not read, that he which made them at the beginning made them male and female, And said, For this cause shall a man leave father and mother, and shall cleave to his wife: and they twain shall be one flesh?' Here a duty, a moral duty, is placed subordinate to a higher moral duty – but yet a duty – nothing romantic, nor yet spiritual. On taking a wife, a man exchanges his filial duty for his marital: to such an extent is this duty developed that there ceases to be any physical division of personality: 'wherefore they are no more twain, but one flesh'.

'Who therefore God hath joined together, let not man put asunder.' This, in fact, sounds not as much a decree against divorce, as a protection from outside human interference within the sacred unity of the marriage bond. This is law. And so, in all justice, the woman must be protected: she may be the property of her husband but he is forbidden to divorce her unless she transgresses by fornication.

As so often, Christ answers the question of marriage in the first place on its own grounds of the Law: He upholds the legality of the marriage law. But then, as ever, He goes further. The Law is never sufficient for it is solely concerned with moral behaviour.

Christ would appear to take marriage as an example: whatever the Law may permit, a second marriage is adulterous. And when His disciples question the severity of this dictum, the reply is as so often: 'All men cannot receive this saying, save they to whom it is given.'

In other words, we are left with the repetitive demand: as Christians to go the step further from legal morality to self-renunciation. It is not the Law which forbids divorce: it remains a personal spiritual battle as with every other obstacle we meet in any attempt to follow the Cross.

'And there be eunuchs, which have made themselves eunuchs for the kingdom of heaven's sake. He that is able to receive it, let him receive it.' Not necessarily a physical eunuch. Adultery can be in the heart with no physical consummation: '... whosoever looketh on a woman to lust after her hath committed adultery with her already in his heart' (*Matthew 5:28*).

Marriage may be *holy* matrimony, and yet, somewhere, somehow, it is still part of the Fall: it is part of 'world': thus, in no way can it be treated as potentially perfect or absolute.

Yes, you must leave father and mother; you are bound morally to each other; you have a duty to each other: but marriage, in itself, is in no way the ultimate, exclusive good. Marriage is necessary: marriage gives many opportunities for spiritual work, for sacrifice, duty to each other, to children. Yet, good as this undoubtedly is, and moreover obviously necessary if the world is to continue, and excellent as marriage is as a safeguard against social anarchy, need it all be taken quite as seriously?

Legal marriage obviously is necessary. Sexual dishonesty is as depraved and culpable as any other dishonesty. Why the pride of place? We should remember the routing of the Sadducees (*Matthew*

22:23ff): 'For in the resurrection they neither marry nor are given in marriage, but are as the angels of God in heaven.'

It might be better not to make an idolatry of marriage lest we exclude what may be following us into eternal life. Yet this does not mean a flaunting of clear issues: adultery not only of the body, but in the heart.

MIRACLES

WHAT ARE MIRACLES? We tend to think of miracles as
opposed to nature – not in the natural order of things
– against the rules of any comprehensible sequence of
events: a reversal of logical development. In other
words, miracles seem a negation of the world as we
know it and we are bewildered because we cannot
explain them: they appear inside our finite world, perceptible, yet in their inception beyond human comprehension. Briefly: miracles are miracles because in
the last count we cannot explain them rationally.

I am speaking here of overt miracles: the blind
seeing, the lame leaping, the lepers cleansed. The fact
that every breath we breathe, every instant of light,
every potato that grows, that the very hairs of our
heads are numbered, are all, all miracles, is not the
immediate theme.

Even to embark on the whole landscape of miracles would mean a life-work, and even then the work
could not be completed. And the writing would in

itself be a miracle! No, when we speak of miracles, we mean not the whole, vast miracle of creation, but, as it were, the miracles within *the* Miracle.

It is very strange. Repeatedly Christ was asked for some proof of His divinity: repeatedly He refused. Yet He performed miracles. And frequently they seemed not only the outcome of divine compassion, but a demonstration of some point of truth.

On one level, the miracles are another form, yet akin to the parables. They teach not in words but in actions. Certain modern educationalists with their affection for 'visual aids' are re-enacting what would seem the same point in teaching. Let them not only hear, but also see: perhaps, then, they will believe.

Matthew 8:2ff: The miracle of the leper, a distinct acknowledgment of the leper's faith: 'if thou wilt, thou canst make me clean'. And Jesus's immediate response to faith: 'I will: be thou clean.'

Matthew 8:5ff: Again faith: the centurion's. But now, in addition to faith, humility. Faith in itself is humility but here we witness not only the faith in Christ's power but also the denial of any value in one-self: we do not merit the gifts of God by any achievement of our own in any realm, worldly or spiritual. It was the centurion's servant who was sick and the centurion, a man of importance, actually sought out Jesus on behalf of his servant: he did not even ask Jesus to come to his home. No wonder Jesus exclaimed, 'I have not found so great faith, no, not in Israel': perhaps one of the first hints of the tragedy awaiting Israel. The servant was healed without even being seen. A visual aid of momentous significance: salvation is not for the Jews alone. Faith has no boundaries either of time or place. Intercession: possibly, the servant did not even know that his master was praying for him.

Matthew 8:14ff: This time no-one interceded, neither relations nor friends, nor did the sick person. Sometimes it seems as if God takes the initiative into His own hands. Why, we do not know. But when Jesus entered Peter's house he healed Peter's wife's mother of her fever. And she 'arose, and ministered unto them'. The love of God can be quite practical. He knows when people are tired and hungry. As long as we are in our human bodies, there is nothing shameful in having bodily needs (cf. wedding at Cana).

Matthew 8:16ff: 'When the even was come, they brought unto him many that were possessed with devils: and he cast out the spirits with his word, and healed all that were sick.' Once again the prodigality of divine love – just like the broadcasting of the seed – how many of those who were healed were good seed? We do not know. But His tender love was unsparing. No doubt much fell by the wayside. It is the visual aid for love that seeks no return. But how Love rejoices when, rarely indeed, someone clings to the goodly pearl!

Matthew 9:2ff: 'They brought him a man sick of the palsy'. *They* brought him. Once again the power of intercession, but this time they actually brought the sick man. It was necessary for him to be present. Perhaps the palsy was the result of some overt sin. But his family's or friends' faith saved him: 'thy sins be forgiven'. In this instance the sins must be forgiven before the healing takes place. And then: 'arise and walk'.

Matthew 9:18ff: This would appear a significant variation from the centurion's servant and the man sick of the palsy: first the intercession: *a certain ruler* begged Jesus to come and lay his hand upon his dead daughter that she might live. This time Jesus accepted the need for His presence. But was there not possibly a further reason for this accepting? He could have healed her as He had healed the centurion's servant, but, if He had, the woman with the issue of blood would not have had the opportunity of approaching Him. And He healed her. Does this suggest that we should not be so immersed in one good work as to ignore another? Did not Jesus go to the ruler's house to illustrate the need for nonexclusiveness even in the urgent pursuit of doing good? And the woman with the issue of blood, does she not perhaps illustrate how, if we have faith, we trust that God always has time for us, however unimportant we may seem compared with others? Christ had time for both: the maid arose and the woman was healed of her plague.

Matthew 9:27ff: The two blind men who followed Him: they again were personally confronted with the confession of His divinity and the healing followed the confession of faith, whereas others brought the dumb man possessed with the devil, and He cast out the devil and the man spoke. In the physical image of bondage, of eyes, ears, tongue, we see the spiritual enslavement to sin: and God's compassionate healing where there is faith.

Matthew 10:8ff: The instructions given to the Apostles when they were sent out by their Master were specific: 'Freely you have received, freely give.' Their miracles of healing, of cleansing lepers, of raising the dead, of casting out devils, were to be the practical illustration of divine love: of divine power entrusted to them. The disciples were blessed by God for this work: they did not assume a sovereignty of their own. They were ordained and sent to imitate precisely what Christ had demonstrated. There was no suggestion of any one of them presuming to choose to go of his own will.

Matthew 12:22ff: The one 'possessed with a devil' was brought to Christ: he was blind and dumb. Christ healed him and the man 'both spake and saw'. Why was this particular man chosen to be cured? The full reason we cannot know, but we do recognize a specific purpose in the circumstances of the healing. There is never to be any question of devilish motivation in what comes from God: there must not be any confusion between the so-called power of evil and the divine power. When the Pharisees suggested that Christ's healing of the man was of the devil, they were routed by the logical reply that if Satan be cast out by the power of Satan, then Satan must become impotent: a kingdom divided against itself. For once and for all we are warned against confusing devilish power, which works and fails in the realm of finite contradiction, and divine power, which is transcendent, and One. Evil fractures. Good unifies.

Matthew 12:43ff: 'When the unclean spirit is gone out of a man ...' After a time the spirit returns, finds everything nice and clean, and resettles, but not only on its own, it brings companions, seven of them 'more wicked than himself'. Confession and absolution, the cleansing, would appear even dangerous if considered passively: as a healing coming from outside and making our sins all nice and clean, passive participation in grace. Yes, the objective grace, the cleansing, in spite of our inadequacy, is certainly there. But work must follow: not a moment to lose. No effort can keep all the devils from returning, but begin again. Unceasing repentance alone will keep the doors as shut as humanly possible against enthusiastic evil.

Matthew 14:14ff: The five thousand were hungry. Jesus had refused Satan's temptation to combat starvation once and for all – if He would worship the Devil. Why then apparently in contradiction did He do precisely what He had so recently refused at the Devil's suggestion? Does this mean, yet once again, that there is no possibility of an absolute answer in this finite world? We are not to claim an absolute or principled answer to questions of the world, but adapt to finite circumstances. Satan's suggestion was a temptation – a temptation, so often repeated, of putting human welfare before God – but if such a temptation is denied, it does not mean that particular cases of human need should be ignored: far from it. It is the principle which Christ knew to be a temptation, and in his refusal to be tempted warned us against such temptation. Principles are dangerous and frequently antipathetic to a condition of repentance: principles can avert our gaze from the presence of evil and deflect us from a recognition of the inevitable presence of evil. But love is another matter. Love is not hampered by mundane logic. Love contradicts and will not be imprisoned by world. Love is not morality. And so, our Lord and Saviour Jesus Christ, as a man tempted in the desert, refused to feed humanity on principle, as the reward for paying homage to the Devil, but, in practice, feeds the hungry lavishly. Once again the prodigality of the Divine Sower – baskets full left over.

Matthew 14:25: 'And in the fourth watch of the night Jesus went unto them, walking on the sea.'

Sometimes, we need reassurance in our faith: the walking on the water was a palpable sign of divinity. But, even more, it surely had the specific purpose of warning Peter. Peter was chosen to have the full weight of the Church on his shoulders: hence, he must first learn his own weakness before he could enter into and strengthen the weakness of the Church to be built on him – the rock. Thus, the walking on the water may be seen as directed to one person, but yet it is capable of wider application.

Is this miracle not a warning to Peter, and for those who followed him as shepherds, not to feel sure of themselves and their unaided power to lead us through tribulation? Again and again, the Litany of Supplication is to accompany Christians: 'Lord, have mercy upon us', and more personal, 'Lord save me.' And to Peter, He stretched out His compassionate hand.

As individuals, we will doubt, we cannot escape it. But for the Church there is no room for discursive deliberation and discussion: 'O thou of little faith, wherefore didst thou doubt?'

Matthew 14:34ff: 'And when they were gone over,

they came into the land of Gennesaret. And when the men of that place had knowledge of him, they sent out into all that country round about, and brought unto him all that were diseased. And besought him that they might only touch the hem of his garment: and as many as touched were made perfectly whole.'

Again, the mystery of the communion of saints: the responsibility is not the heaviest burden always on our own shoulders. We need not feel desolate – isolated – frightened. Somewhere, somehow, others are carrying our burdens.

The initiative did not come from the sick but from those who believed in Him: the sick on this occasion were remarkably passive: we do not even know how much their sickness might have prevented their refusing to come – the extent of their hopelessness. They were *brought*. Intercessory prayer.

Such was the faith of those who brought the sick, that they asked the least possible effort on the part of those whom they brought: merely the minute effort of touching His garment.

The sick were healed. No question was asked as to their faith: nothing to show but the burning love of those who brought them.

Matthew 15:22ff: 'And behold, a woman of Canaan came out of the same coasts.'

We should be careful not to be too grateful that

we are not as others are.

Orthodox; Roman Catholic; Anglican; Nonconformist – we are all privately convinced, however much we discreetly avoid the issue in ecumenical gatherings, that ours is the real Church. Perhaps it is.

Christ did not deny that His chosen people came first. But, first or not first would hardly seem relevant in the context of His love. His Church might remember that, with some spiritual profit!

Matthew 15:30: 'And great multitudes came unto him having with them those that were lame, blind, dumb, maimed, and many others, and cast them down at Jesus's feet; and he healed them.'

Not even, on this occasion, the demand to touch the hem of His garment: a magnificent invitation to the offering up of names in intercession and leaving the solution to Him. Not giving the Almighty precise orders in our prayers: just names, names, names. Throw them at His feet.

Matthew 15:32ff: The feeding of the four thousand follows on their faith in casting at his feet countless sick. They had their reward. He did not send them away fasting.

Even as the sick were healed, so were those who brought them fed. The strength comes, the feeding of the soul, the strength of Christ, even as we may grow weary in prayer.

Matthew 17:14ff: '… A certain man, kneeling down to him, and saying, Lord have mercy on my son, for he is lunatick … And I brought him to thy disciples, and they could not cure him.'

Why could the disciples not cure him? 'Because of your unbelief'. The more 'chosen' we are, the more is demanded of us.

The crowds just brought their sick in their hundreds to Christ – and they were healed – but quite another matter for those appointed to be Christ's representatives. They must die to themselves to be born again in Him before they can begin to carry out His work.

Nothing slick in the work. Nothing mechanical. Every single occasion is as a death and rebirth of faith. Nothing routine, nothing repetitive.

And the divine command for the necessity for prayer and fasting. Not a matter for ratiocination, not part of our religion. But a mystery. To be obeyed as to God Himself not His Church.

Prayer and fasting: an act of love to Christ – irrational – blind. Ultimately, we can only see in blindness – blindness to the rationalism – blindness to the logic of the world. Why pray? Why fast? Our Master ordained it.

Matthew 20:30ff: The two blind men ignored the rebukes of onlookers and persisted in crying for mercy: take no notice in certain circumstances of what seems reasonable or proper, or conventional. Ignore public opinion. Not always, but when we know inwardly that the situation demands a response peculiar to itself.

Interesting to note: sometimes the people bring the sick, sometimes they rebuke the sick for trying to be healed. Individual effort on the whole is not encouraged by the masses.

Sometimes, dare to step out of the herd.

Matthew 21:14: 'And the blind and the lame came to him in the temple; and he healed them.'

What a glorious contrast of wrath and compassion!

He had driven out the hypocrites – the avaricious – the profiteers – the temple was no place for them: and then, the immediate compassion for the sick, the sick who were out of sight, out of hearing, when the temple was busy with the affluent.

Are we to drive out the dead wealth from the temple of our souls, to make room for eternal life?

Matthew 21:18ff: 'Now in the morning as he returned into the city, he hungered. And when he saw a fig tree in the way, he came to it, and found nothing thereon, but leaves only, and said unto it, Let no fruit grow on thee henceforward …'

The fig tree withered and died. How unfair! It was the wrong season. The divine call for service is outside such limitation. It is of no use to quote the laws of nature or man to justify ourselves.

In faith there is no logic. If we fail, we repent, however impossible the divine command may have seemed in the first place: we do not give rational explanations for failure, only repentance is of any use.´

Rational explanations are of the world and perish with the world. Forsake all again and again – in varying forms: mother, father, wife and, so too, the natural sequence of events. Put no reliance on anything temporal. The fig tree did not react in obedience to God. Natural behaviour makes sense for the world. Forsake all, take up your cross, follow me – or wither.

MOTHER OF GOD

Matthew 12:48ff: Who is my mother? and who are my brethren?' Such is the apparent denial of His mother. But, paradoxically, does such denial not emphasize His love and, as man, His human attachment to His mother?

Christ chose no other expression of love for His disciples than identifying them with His mother and brothers. There would seem no stronger, no more emphatic definition of His love. His disciples were for Him as His innermost family.

Hence the explicit reiteration: '… whosoever shall do the will of my Father which is in heaven, the same is my brother, and sister, and mother.' His brother, and sister, and mother – the kernel of family relationship on the human level.

Yet it cannot be some error that this human relationship omits the supposed human father: Christ's divinity is not to be subjected to the slightest possibility of error – even in image for the sake of emphasis.

Joseph is omitted from the family circle – only the Father in heaven is mentioned. Perfect Man – sprung from the root of Jesse through the Virgin Mother and Perfect God – no suggestion of a human father.

Mother of God: bride unwedded – symbol of her divine Son's love for those who followed and would follow Him.

NUMBERS

NUMBERS: a living, consistent, repetitive Christian paradox. Preach to all the world. But (*Matthew 7:16*), give not that which is holy to the dogs. Or again: pearls before swine.

Discrimination is unavoidable as long as we live in a partial world: the absolute, in any form, is not for what is created. Discrimination there must be, but not without compassion and a glad readiness to see the dogs transformed. Yet there would seem no justification for any sentimental palliation of the unclean.

A sower went forth to sow ...: The generous, divine prodigality – seed broadcast indiscriminately – and the inevitable outcome: death, withering, waste.

Swine there will be. Dogs there will be. God, in His divinity, freely will cast His seed everywhere: there is no suggestion of predestination. But there is prodigality: generosity of love.

We are not God. We need not delude ourselves into thinking that we can imitate Him to this extent.

We are limited. We can only work on the smallest piece of ground – perhaps with only the one talent. Such contradiction between the divine and the human narrows our field so that we can work the more freely and intensely. How often we are warned of such limitation!

A Sower: God – Creator – Omnipotent. Yet only the few bore fruit: 'It is given unto you to know the mysteries of the kingdom of heaven, but to them it is not given.'

OATHS/VOWS

SOME PURISTS have great difficulty over the question of vows: should they 'swear' at all? In particular, should they swear the oath in a court of justice?

Christ clearly states (*Matthew 5:34ff*): 'but I say unto you, swear not at all; neither by heaven; for it is God's throne: Nor by the earth; for it is his footstool: neither by Jerusalem; for it is the city of the great King. Neither shalt thou swear by thy head, because thou canst not make one hair white or black. But let your communication be, Yea, yea; Nay, nay: for whatsoever is more than these cometh of evil.'

In fact, this instruction is not concerned with the legal oath – for we are told to render to Caesar what is of Caesar – but it is concerned with our attitude in taking an oath. As truthful people, if we really respect truth, we need not, to put it vulgarly, lay it on thick when we make some assertion in order to convince others of the veracity of our statement: here, we are back once again to the sin of the heart. We need not think that by blustering, by bombastic references to divine attributes, that our veracity will in any wise become more veracious: the truth in the heart needs no adornment.

Examine ourselves severely for the lie in our heart and do not attempt to evade the issue by calling on outside witnesses of the truth of that which is manifestly false.

This has nothing to do with taking an oath in court: the intention there is to frighten us, by the presence of the Bible, into witnessing to the truth as far as we can know it, not only to our fellow men, the human judge, but the Divine Judge. It is not we, in this instance, who are relying on a 'back-up' to our allegations, it is the court, or whatever the legal body concerned, reminding us of the presence of Truth, lest we commit perjury. Such a request from Caesar clearly should be obeyed in the light of Christ's explicit instructions against self-righteous martyrdom.

We have more than enough work to confess Christ in our lives – a life-work of failure and repentance – without taking on extra burdens imposed by unbalanced interpretation of Christ's words.

PEACE

Matthew 11:28–30: Christ's promise of peace for those who follow Him, who are not only Christians by baptism but who seek to live actively by His words. But, what a paradox of peace: 'Come unto me, all ye that labour and are heavy laden, and I will give you rest …'

Labour imposed from outside, forced labour, or labour necessary for physical survival, allows for no rest. But the rest promised by Christ, following labour imposed by Him, takes us into another dimension: another ultimate goal a new concept of proportion. This is the rest from the burden of taking the world around us as the sphere of greatest importance.

Work we must. The Fall demands work. And we must be honest labourers. But, as Christians, we can have something which no immanent hardship or anxiety or even human affection can touch: the peace of the promise beyond this life – the deepest, innermost peace which is totally free from the assaults of the world – 'and I will give you rest'.

The yoke of Christ gives rest not to our bodies but to our souls. This is vital to remember when worldly ills, sickness, persecution, famine, wars, all assail us. What kind of rest is this which we were promised? But this was not the promised rest. The world will never be free of tribulation and it is useless to imagine that it can be. That would surely be falling into Satanic temptation. No, the *heavenly* distinction: 'Ye shall find rest for your *souls*'.

Matthew 10:32ff: The peace of Christ. This inner peace accompanies only a total dedication to Christ. Nothing, no Commandment to honour father and mother, no natural bonds of affection or duty, may stand in the way. The devastating pronouncement: 'For I am come to set a man at variance against his father, and the daughter against her mother …', and not only the family, but so too the family of the peoples: 'Think not that I am come to send peace on earth.' What could be more starkly antagonistic to the Fifth Commandment: 'He that loveth father or mother more than me is not worthy of me …'! (cf. the call of Elisha).

And, when the disciple wished first to bury his father, there came the implacable demand: 'Follow me; and let the dead bury their dead' (*Matthew 8:22*).

Peace? Yes, the peace which can only come when self ceases to torment and cry out for the peace of its own making: the peace *not* of this world.

THE PEOPLE

WHEN SHAKESPEARE WROTE of the people as a many-headed monster, he depicted the crowd in *Julius Caesar*, swayed by the most elementary of oratorical tricks, turning to violence, irrational violence, as the only outlet for their unreasoning emotion: in depicting such a crowd, he was in fact restating dramatically gospel evidence on the same point.

Christ's entry into Jerusalem (*Matthew 21:8ff*) is one of the most tragic events in history, quite apart from its religious inevitability. Of course, His entry, as His subsequent death, were of His own divine will but this did not mitigate the foolish sin: no-one was forced to betray Him. '... and a very great multitude spread their garments in the way ...' What does that teach yet once again?

Beware of popularity, beware of public applause, beware of enthusiastic *numbers*. Two or three gathered together – they are in His Name. Twelve Apostles – sufficient to preach to all the world. But, applauding

crowds – no. The people, in their unreasoning vacilla-
tions, are dangerous. Even the priests feared them,
priests and Pharisees were sufficiently afraid of the
mob not to dare to seize Christ, because at that point
the people 'took him for a prophet'.

Yet this did not last. The same people, terrified
for their own security, were ready to sacrifice Him.
There was no logic in the behaviour, only enthusiasm
followed by frantic reversal into hatred: hardly hatred
even. If only He would show some sign to renew their
enthusiasm, ephemeral as it might prove.

Mindlessness – bewildered sheep, not villains.
But, Christ would not help them. Faith and proof
remain worlds apart. And faith ever needs the consent
of the mind, not the excitement of enthusiasm: the
Cross, not palm branches and triumphant processions.

POVERTY

'LAY NOT UP FOR YOURSELVES treasures upon earth, where moth and rust doth corrupt, and where thieves break through and steal' (*Matthew 6:19*) – strangely enough on one level a practical rather than an immediately spiritual direction.

If we stop to think, it is silly to put all our hopes – our work – our dreams – upon wealth: at any minute the business in which we have invested may go bankrupt, or any of the other calamities we read about in the newspapers or see in all their destructive capacity on television might hit it. Treasures on earth while they last, and we last, seem extremely valuable, but, in the long run, are they such a productive investment? On any level? *Carpe diem*, indeed, for our life span is remarkably short: particularly if we eat off the fat of the land and worry about the stock exchange. Hence, the advice is practical both on the worldly and spiritual level. But what comes next?

'No man can serve two masters: for either he will

hate the one, and love the other: or else he will hold to the one, and despise the other. Ye cannot serve God and mammon' (*Matthew 6:24*). Material wealth is of dangerously vulnerable value, but not only so. There comes the further problem: what is our human capacity for loyalty? Suppose even there were the two masters, more or less of an identical attitude of mind, how could we be in two places at once? On the most elementary level, it is not humanly possible to give full-time service to two employers. We cannot be in two places at once – obviously.

Suppose there were two masters, and the two were diametrically antithetical on every level – suppose, when one says 'go', the other says 'stop', when one applauds, the other derides; when one tells us to go north, the other demands an instant journey south. And if now we emerge from the field of metaphor into spiritual reality, what do we face?

God and world; the divine call and the lure of temporal self-indulgence; our vision set on heaven and our ambition worldly success: wholly incompatible; not even uneasy partners; no compromise possible – 'Ye cannot serve God and mammon.'

This contradiction, world and spirit, is emphasized to the uttermost in the lack of concern demanded for physical wellbeing. We are still in the realm of metaphor as we rise to the climax of anti-world: 'Take no thought for your life, what ye shall eat, or what ye shall drink; nor yet for your body, what ye shall put on. Is not the life more than meat, and the body than raiment?'

Here we meet the extreme point of antithesis to the serving of mammon: far from attempting to accumulate unnecessary wealth, we must not even be concerned for essentials. Of course we must be: we are not meant to see our families starving or begging. But, and this surely is the point, the clothing and feeding of ourselves, our families, our monastic communities, should not be an end in itself – should not become something to serve and worship: 'Ye cannot serve God and mammon.'

Animals – birds – are incapable of logical argument, yet they do not starve: they would appear the extreme antithesis to overconcern. There is no harm, only obvious instinctive good, in a bird's care for its nestlings, human or otherwise. But not as the prime, the ultimate, the transcendent aim.

The theme of poverty persists into the evangelical field: the disciples must have trust. Sent out on their missionary journeys (*Matthew 10:9*) directed to preach and to heal, yet they are to take no money, no extra clothing. Why? Perhaps the answer lies in a double movement: not only that they should be free from any inclination to serve mammon, but also that indirectly they might influence those whom they were to teach, in as much as the people, with worldly possessions, should be responsible for those giving their whole time to serving God: 'the workman is worthy of his meat'.

Thus, although none of us should serve God and mammon in the ultimate sense, there is nothing, as always, absolute in the divine command. Some must work and earn – without worshipping the earnings – and others must, as far as possible, in God's Name, not from indolence, devote their time away from the world, but for the spiritual care of the workers.

As for the rich young man (*Matthew 19:21*), he really thought that he deserved a passport to heaven. But he failed the final test: 'If thou wilt be perfect, go and sell that thou hast, and give to the poor, and thou shalt have treasure in heaven: and come and follow me.' Is there a touch of irony here? The rich young man dared to think that he qualified for heaven: he was too rich – rich in money did not matter as much, but rich in self-approval was another matter – so he was put to the ultimate test: to sell everything and give to the poor. Of course he could not. But perhaps if he had not been as sure of his own integrity he would not have been put to public shame, and forced to slip away disgraced. Just being rich in money need not have excluded him from heaven: 'with God all things are possible'. The wealth of self-righteousness is another matter.

Perhaps with the question of poverty, there comes an unexpected slant – the essential purpose of the community of saints: what one cannot do, the other can. We cannot all be poor. We cannot all help the poor. Someone will always be poor, someone rich, in one way or another. But whatever each one of us lacks, another has. How dreadful is the very thought of being in the truest sense absolutely alone: but we are not. When we are poor in prayer, others pray. When we are poor in charity, others give. And such a belief, far from leading to complaisance, is a never-ceasing spur – we cannot know what contribution is demanded from us within the communion. We must work without ceasing, knowing that whatever we give will never be adequate. Poverty.

PRAYER

Matthew 6:6ff: Pray secretly. Prayer is a mystery. A mystery between us and God. In a way, we even pray secretly from ourselves – only God knows what is really in our hearts. He rewards openly. Some of the meaning is revealed by Him – not by us. And we may not even recognize the revelation because it will be His – not ours.

Matthew 6:7: '… use not vain repetition'. Again, a mystery. God alone knows what is vain – empty – meaningless, and what is ceaseless importunity. We have been told to knock and knock and knock again. The widow was rewarded for her importunity. It is vain repetition that is at fault. Prayer repeated for the sake of pious effect. Otherwise, (*Matthew 7:7ff*) – ask – seek – knock. Pray. 'To him that knocketh it shall be opened.'

'And all things, whatsoever ye shall ask in prayer, believing, ye shall receive' (*Matthew 21:22*). True prayer is a meeting of the human will with the divine.

Such prayer is already answered although we do not know it: we are groping our way, in prayer, to meet the divine end. There is no time in this context but, if there were, prayer *follows*, not precedes.

Christ and His Father were One. We, sinful creatures, are, as far as we know, connected by prayer, which is put into our hearts by the Spirit. Hence, prayer is a giving back to God of His own, according to our individual measure. Thus, prayer is answered because true prayer is essentially of His will. 'Not my will.'

Prayer is repentance: and listening. Paradise was made of peace, and so Adam could hear the divine voice. It is more difficult now. Christ, Himself, (*Matthew 14:23*) withdrew apart to a mountain that He might pray. But we need also to withdraw from the turmoil within ourselves.

Liturgical prayer is also blessed. '… where two or three are gathered together in my name …' He is there. And, again, He inspires us. We, in prayer, can achieve nothing of our own – only return to Him, His inspiration within the measure of our limitation. Repentance.

PROOFS

FROM THE VERY BEGINNING, in the presence of the living Christ, people demanded proof.

Faith has rarely been recognized as a positive integration of doubt: again and again, for their faith people have demanded tangible evidence, not realizing the mutual exclusion of proof and faith. If there is proof, then no faith is possible. It is faith that is demanded of Christians, not the acceptance of some fact, or the persistent seeking for a logical foundation for Christianity. It is strange that over all these centuries, in one form or another, we have perpetuated the cry of the Pharisees and Sadducees and 'desired him that he would shew them a sign from heaven' (*Matthew 16:1*). It is never quite clear whether we long for proof in order that our own faith might leave the realm where we cannot rationally defend it to ourselves or others, or that we simply long for it, in some strange way, as a divine assertion. We want God to assert Himself in a sovereign manner, so that we can, as it were, point Him out proudly: 'Look – now you must agree that our God is a great God.' And that is precisely what He refused to do. He did not summon hosts of angels to His assistance. He was not born in the royal palace. His journey on a donkey can be interpreted in more than one way. His armies had only twelve leaders, of whom one betrayed Him, and the other eleven fled, albeit temporarily. His followers hid in secret meeting places and catacombs. And most of His people were far from noble.

'Master, we would see a sign from thee …' Even those who instinctively loved and followed Him, yet wanted proof: did He or did He not legally fulfil the prophetic utterances of the coming of the Messiah? But consistently He refused the snare in the path of doubt. His followers must learn the path of faith: they must accept the difference between faith and knowledge – for how can the human mind grasp the shape of the divine?

Knowledge of God is not possible. Proof is impossible. Yet they continued, and continue to ask – some truly humbly, some in derision as in Jerusalem of old – 'Master, we would see a sign from thee.' So now, throughout the world. Yet, now, how often is there even a request for a sign? It is more a careful ironing out of anything which gives Christianity its unique validity. There is no sign to justify His personal 'superiority' over Buddha or Krishna or Mohammed. Yet there was a sign: '... the sign of the prophet Jonas ...'

Resurrection – not out of the belly of the whale but out of hell – the destruction of death by death. Yet, there again, we can only accept the Resurrection by faith, not by proof. Either we fall down before Him in recognition, breathing the tender 'Rabboni' with Mary Magdalene, or we devise contradictory tales to explain rationally the disappearance of His body.

Proof is not the point. Faith is.

PROPHETS

Matthew 7:15ff: 'Beware of false prophets ... ye shall know them by their fruits.'

This is indeed an exciting thought, branching out into a very wilderness of connotations. First of all, we are to beware of false prophets. We must not rely on innate good sense to recognize the false and their teaching. We must not be confident that we can discern good from evil as easily as black from white: we need to be constantly on our guard. And, avoid entering into argument either in the hope of convincing the adversary or justifying ourselves.

But, if we are not to be drawn into discussion, how then are we to recognize the innate lie? Quite simply: 'by their fruits'. Here emerges another facet of faith and works: faith without works is empty idealism, works without faith are not necessarily Christian.

If the prophet, the teacher, the missionary, is a true prophet, so will his works be: where we cannot be sure of a man by his words, we can become more sure when we see how his behaviour matches his sentiments.

'*Beware of false prophets*': not necessarily those outside, but, much more dangerous, the 'prophets' within ourselves: careful self-scrutiny before all else. Know ourselves: fear our own fruits. 'Not everyone that saith unto me, Lord, Lord, shall enter into the kingdom of heaven ...' (*Matthew 7:21*).

Others – but ourselves first of all. There is nothing, no-one to be more feared than the evil lodged in our own hearts: and deflecting the guilt upon the false prophets outside will not save us.

It is for us to eschew wrong doctrine from within ourselves, to build our house upon a rock: *the* Rock.

REPENTANCE

REPENTANCE IS NOT to be confused with feeling sorry towards another man: repentance is a measure of oneself in the face of God.

Repentance takes us out of the moral realm into the spiritual. The dividing line, as always, is hardly to be defined and perhaps in practice not discernible – it is once again the First Commandment 'spilling over' into the Second. But, as in all spiritual work, the act of repentance is hidden. The yeast in the dough. The prodigal son repented: he realized that he had sinned 'before heaven' and before his father – but heaven came first (*Luke 15:18*).

Matthew 21:23ff: The chief priests and the elders asked Jesus, 'By what authority doest thou these things? and who gave thee this authority?' In reply, they were told the parable of a man and his two sons. One refused to work in his vineyard, but repented, and went to work; one said that he would go, and did not: in image, the repenting publicans and harlots and the chief priests who would not recognize Christ for who He was. Priests and Pharisees remained obdurate, even as the elder of the two sons in the parable: they too, by their very calling and position, in effect had said 'I go', but had remained fastened in the letter of the Law: while the sinners repented. Repentance: work in the vineyard, at whatever hour.

Once again the vineyard (*Matthew 21:33ff*). The husbandmen, the priests, the Pharisees, the lawyers, clung on to their Master's land. No question of repentance even in the face of His Son. Here is the full horror of non-repentance: they were the *trusted* leaders of God's chosen people – yet, in the face of God Incarnate they only cared for their own security and position. The letter of the Law: fasting, praying, charity, but – no repentance.

And the converse: Peter. He, who knew Jesus, who loved Him as a man, and believed in Him as God. Peter, who had been chosen to witness His Transfiguration. Peter, who had sworn fealty. Peter – in sudden and overpowering personal fear – betrayed Him (*Matthew 26:69ff*). 'Then began he to curse and to swear, saying, I know not the man.' But, his repentance was to God: his bitter weeping the prelude to action – martyrdom. The rock on which the Church was built is unassailable, for is it not built on the safest of foundations – repentance?

SALVATION

'BUT MANY THAT ARE FIRST shall be last; and the last shall be first' (*Matthew 19:30*).

Why is it that instinctively we all tend to identify ourselves with those who surprisingly attain to heaven? We are the publican, the lost sheep saved, the piece of money found – somehow in seeming humility we carry pride to the furthermost limit. Confessing our inadequacy, thereby we creep through the back door of adequacy. So perhaps salvation will come even more unexpectedly to those who really appear to have deserved it – if anyone can deserve anything. We are ever in the paradoxical world of uncertainty – when is the Pharisee the publican and when the publican the Pharisee?

Contradictions pursue us:

Matthew 7:13: 'Enter ye in at the strait gate … strait is the gate, and narrow is the way which leadeth unto life, and few there be that find it …' Yet, *Matthew 18:11* may well sound reassuring: 'The Son of man is come to save that which was lost … if a man have an hundred sheep …' He will leave the ninety-nine safe ones and make every effort to find the lost one. Does this suggest that we cannot find our own salvation? We may even lose ourselves if we rely upon ourselves to find the way through the narrow gate: we certainly must try, but can we do it? Should we not follow the flock (the Church?) rather than pursuing an individual (dissident) path, and getting lost?

Does not Christ wish to lead us out of the hope of individual, privately designed salvation into the one way – salvation in the Church founded by Him? The straying sheep need not have been the overt sinner – it could as well have been the self-righteous or mistaken one who trusted in himself to find the best pasture: for him, perhaps, it was the flock which was on the wrong path. He considered reformation essential, and he hoped to lead the way – into the wilderness of schism.

Matthew 19:16ff: 'Good Master, what good thing shall I do, that I may have eternal life?' Here is a sheep, not obediently within the flock, nor yet by self-will outside it, but, as it were, hovering between the two, wishing to make a self-determined choice: not willing to give in, to surrender his right to choose. He cannot sell everything, but must retain some mastery over his own destiny. His wealth makes it seem impossible to reach the Kingdom of Heaven: such a narrow gate.

And his camel burdened and made wide with all his possessions – not necessarily bad possessions – but, yet, the outcome of determined self-will.

The rich young man and the lost sheep, in effect, are one and the same. Is there no hope for them? But the good Shepherd seeks out the self-sufficient sheep, and, as for the rich young man, the same applies to him: he cannot find the right way on his own, even as the sheep could not, but the Shepherd in His infinite love can perform miracles of rescue work: 'With God all things are possible.'

Yet it remains a great difficulty to grasp the essential sin – not of doing perceptible evil, but of ostracizing oneself by virtuous aloofness, relying on one's own spiritual possessions and potentialities and ignoring the straight and narrow path established by God Himself and preserved in the one fold, the Church.

SELF-SACRIFICE

SACRIFICE IS DEMANDED. Sacrifice of our nearest and dearest is even conceivable, so too sacrifice of affluence, but, what of sacrifice of ourselves?

Matthew 10:39: 'He that findeth his life shall lose it; and he that loseth his life for my sake shall find it.'

Now we are being tested as by fire. To sacrifice others is still another demand from deliberately, rationally, without the encouragement of ecstasy or public applause, sacrificing ourselves.

What did Satan hope from Job? Did Satan not boast to God, 'touch his bone and his flesh, and he will curse thee to thy face' (*Job 2:5*)? Did not Christ's own beloved disciples flee in terror at the moment of His arrest? And Peter? It was no accident that the ordained Rock of the Church was as sand before the fear of martyrdom – but only for the shortest of time. This spasm of self-preservation is recorded perhaps to help us in our weakness to gain the strength of love – as Peter did – through the mighty strength of repentance.

But that is what is demanded. Not sacrifice of wealth, position, family, one's native land, but our lives – our lives for life or death as God wills. 'And he that taketh not his cross and followeth after me, is not worthy of me.' The personal cross – whatever is demanded of us – ultimately our lives. Our lives for martyrdom. Witness.

What we say or do, through baptism, we say and do as Christians. But, a Christianity unrealized: a baptism unfulfilled in action.

Self-sacrifice to Christ – fulfilment of faith in speech and in deed – positive negation of self.

SPEECH

'FOR BY THY WORDS thou shalt be justified, and by thy words thou shalt be condemned' (*Matthew 12:37*).

And again: 'Whosoever therefore shall deny me before men, him will I also deny before my Father which is in heaven' (*Matthew 10:32*).

Why are words of such importance?

So often in the world words are sneered at as hot air. Action is constantly demanded. But if the soul, and not the body, is at stake, then words are of a terrifying importance.

Words express our thinking. Words are the medium for communication. Words are the reflection of truth or falseness. Words can damn us where there is no question of action.

How else should we sin against the Holy Spirit other than in the blasphemy of denying the Divine Trinity? Denying the divinity of Christ? 'That which cometh out of the mouth, this defileth a man' (*Matthew 15:11*).

The unforgivable sin is the sin against the Holy Spirit, and this sin, spoken out loud, or spoken silently in the secret places of the heart, can only take the form of words, for words are the medium of our thoughts, even though not expressed aloud.

THE SWORD

'AND BEHOLD, one of them which was with Jesus stretched out his hand, and drew his sword, and struck a servant of the high priest's, and smote off his ear. Then said Jesus unto him, Put up again thy sword into his place: for all they that take the sword shall perish with the sword.'

Is this an unequivocal prohibition against any form of military activity? Have we at last something clear and definite to follow? A divine instruction? Surely this is the command to herald in pacificism? Perhaps. But perhaps not.

Could this command not be a suggestion of the futility of defending Christ from His self-chosen sacrifice? It might well seem that yet again we are forbidden the dangerous luxury of an absolute command within our finite flux.

What follows? 'Thinkest thou that I cannot now pray to my Father, and he shall presently give me more than twelve legions of angels?'

How dare we attempt to defend Christ God from His chosen way? How dare we presume to defend with our paltry swords the Incarnate God? The natural inclination to defend the Beloved is in fact a denial of His sovereign dominion.

We indeed perish by the sword, we are mortal: but Christ, by His death, trampled down death. We need no longer rely on the sword for survival – and perish. We live in Him.

TEMPTATION

TEMPTATION HAS BEEN BLESSED. There was no apparent need, certainly on the human level, for Christ deliberately to go into the wilderness to be tempted. 'Then was Jesus led up of the spirit into the wilderness to be tempted of the devil.' He was led up 'of the spirit': the Holy Spirit; the Spirit of Truth.

As man, temptation cannot be avoided; as God, it can be faced on the divine level. Thereby we surely learn that temptation, unavoidable as it is, can be met provided we make no effort to answer the Devil on his own terms: we can only safely meet temptation by ignoring the deceptively good grounds of the temptation and keeping strictly to the narrow path of austere truth. Temptation would not be temptation if it did not, at least superficially, seem good. It may be easy to deny overt evil, but not as easy to deny something which, at first glance, is attractively generous. Only poverty can help: poverty even towards the wealth of being a benefactor.

Christ was faced by the most alluring of temptations: to overcome poverty – thereby to prove His divinity and remove the terror of doubt from the world – and to become avowed Sovereign of the whole inhabited earth. He refused. Good cannot come out of evil. If 'good' needs subservience to the Devil, then it is not good. And the wellbeing of this life – in this world – however laudable an aim, is not the final aim. The Devil's temptations were a demand to betray the truth for temporal wellbeing: homage to what is transitory at the expense of the eternal.

Temptation emanates from evil, but so too from sincere love (*Matthew 16:22*). Peter wanted to protect Christ from the destined purpose of His Incarnation: his love only saw the immediate injury to his beloved Master. Such protective love was misplaced – temptation: 'Get thee behind me, Satan.' Peter, from love of Christ, sought to keep Him tied to the world, even as the Devil had done from hatred and fear – temptation of protectiveness.

Temptation, at its worst, is for 'good' – it is easy to discern temptation for evil – if not easy to avoid it.

WOMEN

THE *COURAGE* OF THE WOMEN, some without names, shines radiantly throughout the Gospel. Such courage could only emanate from faith in the One they followed. Not the faith of doctrine. Not debatable faith. Not a creed, but warm, living, personal love: the love towards a person, somehow recognized as a Person. And this person/Person not to be dogmatized over but to be followed, served, loved.

At the point of crucifixion, at the moment of personal danger for His followers, the men fled. The disciples deserted their Master. But (*Matthew 27:55*) '... many women were there beholding afar off, which followed Jesus from Galilee'. Amongst them was Mary Magdalene. Mary Magdalene – who was she, so chosen that she would be the first to recognize the Risen Christ?

Mary Magdalene, in some ways, was to be seen some centuries later in her namesake, St Mary of Egypt. Both had this immense, devouring power of love in them. Both began by focusing the love in what we would consider a sinful direction. Both redirected their love – one on the actual presence of Christ, the other in her heart. What can be more alien from love than a prostitute's sale of her body? The mystery is unfathomable. Yet it was St Mary of Egypt who went into the desert to parched heat, freezing cold, starvation, and it was St Mary Magdalene and 'the other Mary' who sat at the sepulchre and at dawn, at the very first moment permitted by the Law, came to the tomb. To them was granted the vision of the angel, and the glory of the message entrusted to them. The glory of the overcoming of death, the glory of the salvation of the world: 'go quickly, and tell his disciples that he is risen from the dead'.

The women were given the message, and the women *believed*: the first to believe in the Risen Christ. What a heritage for all women of the future! But, surely, a *defined* heritage? The women were to tell the disciples: the Apostolic succession. And the women did not question their own significance: they had the news confirmed by the Risen Christ who met them on the way. And He repeated the instruction: 'Be not afraid: go tell my brethren that they go into Galilee.' The women were given the greatest honour. And this, this particular honour, was sufficient for them.

WORLD

Matthew 6:24: 'No man can serve two masters: for either he will hate the one, and love the other; or else he will hold to the one, and despise the other. Ye cannot serve God and mammon.'

Ye *cannot*: not, you must not, you should not, it is preferable not to, it is sinful to attempt both. No. Simply, you *cannot*. Starkly, it is not possible.

God and mammon draw in diametrically opposite, and opposing, directions: the physical image of the impossibility of going north and south at the same instant illustrates the spiritual deadlock.

The choice must be made. We can slither about, sidling towards one, then to the other, but thereby achieving neither so-called success in the world nor even the first step towards a life divorced from every aspect of worldly riches. And not only riches.

The point is driven home to the uttermost. We might congratulate ourselves quite justifiably that we are not concerned with wealth, that we are satisfied with our modest standard of life, not covetous, honest, good husbands and wives, mothers and fathers, regular churchgoers: all this, surely is not serving mammon. Yet, the next step demanded may well prove harder.

We might call it prudence, and possibly the care for the next day's food and clothing for our families, for ourselves, our communities, is only sensible: even birds build their nests and rabbits their burrows. Must such providence also go? '...Take therefore no thought for tomorrow.' In practical terms, an impossible command. In its very impossibility a reminder of our final inadequacy, a loving passport to repentance: we not only are not, but we cannot, be worthy.

Whatever we do is inadequate. It is not possible to serve God and mammon, but mammon, in some form, is unavoidable. We cannot serve God. But He serves us. He washes our feet. He gives us His body and blood for the food and drink which does not perish. And, whatever else, we need not confuse *real* world and *transient* world.

Real world lies within us – within our own finite natures – in the inner call to survive and protect – to feed and to give to drink – to plan for the future: the estimable qualities which, somehow, must yet not take priority in our hearts and yet be fulfilled.

Unreal world is the world it is so easy to avoid by

having principles to which we attempt to adhere absolutely. It is such a soothing balm to make an act of self-willed conscience an objective obedience to God: hence we are sharply reminded of *true* values. It is not 'world' in our hearts when tribute money is demanded by the government in one form or another. Such a demand comes from outside, it is connected with the daily existence from which we cannot escape in this life. It is trivial. So, let us catch a fish and pay the tribute 'lest we should offend them'. 'Render therefore unto Caesar' what belongs to Caesar. World to world.

Do not imagine that you are serving God by disobedience to the law of the realm. No, the sin is *in* our heart. *World* is in our heart: temptation, ambition, lust, hatred. The inner tribute money paid to Evil. We cannot shed the guilt lightly by means of complacent denial of the laws of the land. Where the superscription is Caesar's, give it due service. But not *the* service.

Above all, *the* service is far from conducive to self-satisfaction and moral complacency, *the* service is a tormenting dilemma which can never be fully resolved. Whom shall I feed? My child or yours? There *is* no final answer – only repentance – let us begin again.

And ambition? The mother of James and John wanted them to sit one on the right and the other on the left of the Master in the Kingdom of Heaven: surely a laudable desire and one not of this world? Surely not the wish to serve God and mammon? – but yet, – world. The values of the world. As it were earthly status transferred by a loving mother to heavenly. Even her love, in its exclusiveness for her sons, was *world*. There might be tribulation in the world, but she envisaged a heavenly reward for her sons in exchange for present poverty – and she was not the last to do so. Yet, clearly, comes the answer: not only in heaven, but already in this world we must readjust our ideas. You cannot serve God and mammon.

'… whosoever will be great among you, let him be your minister; And whosoever will be chief among you, let him be your servant.' All prestige is taken from us. We should have nowhere to lay our heads, but we have. And we need to have, for physical survival. Again and again the paradox of imperfection.